MILK
FROM
SAND

A child in communist Russia, from WWII to 1960

Leonila V. Montgomery

Opus
SELF-PUBLISHING
WASHINGTON, DC

Published though Opus Self-Publishing Services
Located at:
Politics and Prose Bookstore
5015 Connecticut Ave. NW
Washington, D.C. 20008
www.politics-prose.com / / (202) 364-1919

CONTENTS

To my sister, Svetlana, who saved my life,
who took care of me from my early childhood,
whose beauty was in her big, dark-blue eyes
and her large soul.
I love you, and I will remember you
forever.

Lilia

Prologue

My husband Paul and I were driving from Boston towards Ohio to visit his mother Elizabeth. We talked and laughed, never bored because we had in our past and present such different cultural roots, customs, events, and perspectives on the world. Even simple questions like "Paul, did you always have sugar in the stores, even in your childhood, even during the War?" put us immediately into such different parts of the planet Earth--one in America, the other 12,000 miles away in Russia. I tried to tell Paul some short stories from my life and he tried to record in this book whatever I remembered. The memories came suddenly to me, hidden somewhere deep in my head, appearing in dreams that were frightening at times and unexplained, but always with a bit of sadness. The stories are not chronological, not judgmental, not criticizing; Anna Akhmatova called such memories "black memories." For me, they are scattered pieces of a childhood in communist Russia during WWII and through the 50's.

MILK *FROM* SAND

1

Under the Shed (1941)

I am Lilia.

In the late spring of 1941 when I was two, my family and I left Moscow to vacation with my grandparents in Urovichy, a remote village in the republic of Byelorussia close to Poland. We all arrived at the small house of my grandparents on the edge of the village. The house was shrouded by bushes and trees, with an animal shed on the other side of Grandma's kitchen garden. Behind the shed, the land sloped down through brush to a river.

Grandpa was not very talkative that evening and was not very glad to see us. At supper, the first thing he said to my mom was, "Maria, I think you are a smart young woman. Do not think that I'm not glad to have you and your kids here. But we are very close to the German border, and war is in the air. Only idiots do not understand that."

My grandma started screaming back at him in a high-pitched voice, "Oh, man, why do you consider yourself smarter than Stalin and Molotov? Didn't you see in the newspaper the photograph of our Molotov with the highest level of German generals? Everyone says the Germans are our best friends and that no war with Germany will occur. It's forbidden even to talk about war, or do you want to go to prison?"

Grandma wanted to scream something more, but my nine-year-old brother, Anatoly, whom we called Tolya, suddenly interrupted her. He had recently become a Pioneer (like the Scouts in structure but with Communist content) and wore a red bandana, and his shirt had a red star with Lenin's picture inside the star worn over his heart. He declared, "My dad said that war is inevitable, and you, woman, just shut up. My dad is a teacher. He knows everything, and he also said that these Bolshevik bastards have fooled us again and again." Grandma started laughing loudly and uncontrollably. Mom grasped Anatoly and started to beat him, ordering him never to tell anybody that again. He promised right away; and Grandma shouted at Grandpa that he had spoiled the family supper. My seven-year-old sister Svetlana hid under the table, and I started crying loudly and wouldn't stop. Grandma grabbed her long oven paddle and started to beat Grandpa, who ran away outside and didn't come home until late at night.

The next morning I went to the animal shed on the other side of Grandma's garden. Through the cracks in its log walls, I could see a few pigs and cows moving around making sudden animal sounds. Across the river was a forest.

Grandmother Anna was famous in her little village as a healer. She could stop seizures and bleeding and calm down people who were crying. She was showing me how to collect roots and leaves as her grandmother had shown her. My father, Vladimir, a history teacher, yelled at her to stop. "Don't ruin her scientific understanding with that nonsense!" Grandma replied, "Modern medicine will never go higher than ancient medicine. Everything is in the plants!"

There were pictures in the newspapers of two men hugging, the same pictures we had seen in Moscow. My mother told me it was Stalin and Hitler, that they were friends and would never fight. Only my father talked openly about a war coming. "In June!" he kept saying. On June 22, 1941, war broke out. My father and other teachers in the area were sent to a military camp to learn how to train new officers, since Stalin had killed so many or put them in jail. The next day, Germans occupied our village, and we were cut off from the rest of the world.

German soldiers began visiting homes, and people began disappearing. This made the villagers desperate to cooperate with the invaders. Our Moscow accents and dark hair made us bigger prizes for the Germans.

Plus, the villagers in general hated the Central Government in Moscow. So when someone Grandma didn't trust came to the house, she sent me and my older brother and sister down to the dirt basement. From there we crawled through a little tunnel under the garden and ended up below the animal shed in a storage space which Grandma used for hiding harvested potatoes and vegetables from Stalinist troops collecting "agricultural tax."

In the fall, my older brother Tolya saw a group of people being led past the house. He thought it was a parade, like in Moscow, so he ran out and started marching and singing. A local policeman who knew Grandma pushed his rifle against Tolya's chest and said in a low voice, "Tolya, go home now!" Tolya wanted to stay for the excitement. The policeman finally got rough and pushed him into the bushes on the side of the road. Tolya ran home crying to Grandma that the policeman wouldn't let him join the demonstration. In horror, she beat him with a towel and told him never to leave the house again. That night, when we saw bodies floating down the river, our mother Maria vowed to join the Resistance Movement; my Father had done so earlier. It was a momentous decision for the family.

In Russia, to be ready for a trip is to have enough vodka. So Grandpa decided to brew Mother a barrel before she left. She would have enough vodka to keep her warm, to clean wounds, and to share with her fellow Resistance fighters.

He spent the afternoon peeling beets and potatoes and tossing them into a barrel of water on the porch. He added the yeast and brought the barrel into the warm kitchen. Wide-eyed, I watched him place it on a little bench. He picked me up and put me on top of the high Russian oven where I could see everything. I watched Grandpa bustling about the kitchen, adding things to the brew and occasionally pinching my knee. My mother sat at the table, somber and quiet. Grandma gave her a warm sheepskin coat she had made.

Grandpa was a power that night. I couldn't take my eyes off of him. When he went out to the hallway shelves to fetch another ingredient, I leaned so far out to watch that I fell from the top of the oven right into the

3

vodka barrel. It tipped over and spread the floor with a layer of beets, potatoes, and one sopping Lilia! My mother grabbed me and rushed me outside, alarmed as I was. She was afraid her father would beat me.

"It is a bad sign," he said, "a bad sign to leave home without vodka." He left immediately but came back later that evening with a large jar of home-brew he had gotten from a neighbor. Grandma Anna was giving Mother some last-minute nursing advice; she reminded Mother about putting sphagnum, a dry moss, on resistance fighters' wounds to prevent infection.

Late that night, my mother said goodbye to me and set out to find the local underground partisans. She took my brother and my sister with her, but didn't take me because I was so small and the trip would be long and cold.

After they were gone, Grandma immediately stashed me in the hideout under the shed. The smell of the hay and the animals was strong and comforting. But after a few days, grandma slaughtered the animals so the Germans couldn't take them.

Three days later, my sister Svetlana came back looking cold and worried. She said mother had made contact with someone at the edge of a wide river, someone who would take her to the partisans. But the contact said Svetlana was too small and weak and might die crossing the river. So mother sent her back and went on with my brother to join the partisans.

Grandma was afraid for Svetlana and me, afraid that the Germans would take us off to prison. She made us stay under the shed and constantly told us never to say anything for fear our Moscow accents would draw the attention of the Germans. Svetlana was sometimes allowed to go up into the house and do chores when Grandma thought it was safe. And sometimes, at night, I was allowed to come up for a few hours to get warm and stretch. My grandfather had stopped being affectionate with me after I spilled the vodka. He only repeated that I should never say anything, lest I be recognized as a Moscow child with Moscow parents.

Months passed. Each day I wondered what was happening to Mother and Anatoly. On the day before my fourth birthday, I awoke to hear

Svetlana running out of Grandma's bedroom where we had slept that night, calling for Grandma. When I caught up to them, she was telling Grandma her dream. "I was walking in the middle of the night, walking and walking. It was very dark, but I was carrying three lit candles. The wind was blowing the flames back and forth and almost put them out, but I kept walking and they stayed lit." Grandma fell to her knees and crossed herself. "Thank God, they are safe," she said. "They may be wounded, but all three will come home safely."

That evening, in Grandma's bedroom, Svetlana said to me, "Let's pretend Mommy comes to get us, okay? Do you want to play, Lilia?"

"Yes! Yes!" I said.

But first Svetlana sternly shook her finger right at my nose and said, "Don't forget it's a game; I'm warning you. Remember, this is just a game. Do you swear you won't forget? I don't want you crying and squeaking. Okay? It's just a game." And she went out of the room and closed the door.

I sat and stared at the door, and then I heard a knock.

"Who's there?" I called out softly.

A voice something like my mother's answered, "This is Maria Ilyushenko from the Resistance Movement, and I've come back to take my children home to Russia. May I come in?" And the door opened slowly while my eyes opened wider and wider.

When I saw that it was Svetlana and not my mother, I started to cry and cry. Svetlana immediately resumed her own voice and tried to shush me: "Be quiet! Be quiet! Grandma will hear you. Please shut up. It was only a game. You promised." I cried on and on, only softer so no one would hear.

Meanwhile, Grandma continued to receive villagers coming to her for healing. One day a local policeman came and demanded a picture of my mother. He said she was suspected of being a partisan. My grandmother picked up the baking paddle she used to put bread in the oven, and beat him several times with it. When he retreated, she said in a low, intense voice, "Sure, you can take the picture. Go ahead. But I will spoil and damage your family for ten generations. Go into the living room, take the picture, but know that your family will be harmed for ten generations. You know I can do it. And if you kill me, I will do it from the grave."

The policeman left quickly: "Forget I was here. Please, never mention that I was here, and do not remember what I said to you. Please forget I was here."

I lived under the shed all during the war. Grandma fed me potatoes, onions, fresh-baked bread and a lot of garlic that kept me from being sick. Svetlana occasionally talked to me, but I mostly stayed quiet, just as my grandparents ordered. The only clothes we had were burlap dresses my grandmother made and some other rags. We were cold most of the time and thought a lot about food. But in the spring and summer, I sometimes crawled through the brush behind the shed and sat lazily in the warm sunlight, looking down to the river and across at the forest, imagining my mother cooking in Moscow and my father fighting the Fascists.

One winter evening Grandma let us come into the house to sleep. Late at night she woke us up, saying she had heard a knock on the outside wall. "Oh my God, oh my God," she said at first. "But... no, that is a light knock. The Germans always knock loudly and firmly." She left us quietly, and I went back to sleep.

I awoke to conversation from the kitchen. Two men were talking with Grandma at the table with a little candle burning. The window was blocked with a big blanket. One man was smiling with Svetlana on his lap. He had a special hat and a shiny belt around his green uniform, and he said, "Oh, Lilia's awake. Lilia, come here."

"Noooo." I was afraid of everybody. My grandmother had told me not to go to anyone. The man whispered, "Lilia, come here. I am your father. I have come to see you, to see if you are all right."

"Noooo... My father is beating fascists." Grandma was shocked, because she had taught me never to respond, to say at most, "I don't know," but certainly nothing about fascists! But I had answered strongly and in a deep voice, sure and proud of this father. The man motioned again for me to come to him. I just plopped down on the kitchen floor. He tried to pick me up. I shrieked and cried. Grandma said, "Don't touch her then. She will just cry louder and louder." She knew me very well.

My father sat and looked at me, at my face, at my burlap dress. He stood to go, reached into his military bag and pulled out two shirts and said to Grandma, "Mom, sew dresses for them from these." Then he and his sergeant rode off into the night on their horses. Grandma gave the shirts to our Aunt Vera in neighboring Mozor, who sewed them into two clean dresses for us.

In the spring of 1944, the Russian Red Army was approaching our village, so the Germans began packing everything up. An order was given to round up all the children without parents and send them to a camp in Mozor.

My grandmother was away from the house looking for food, and Svetlana and I were under the shed. We heard soldiers and the voice of the local policeman Grandma had threatened with a curse, and then suddenly we were discovered.

They put us into the back of a military truck with some other children. I was silent the whole time. Svetlana was trembling and screaming hysterically, "Grandpa! Grandpa!" But he was very deaf and did not hear. The soldiers said we'd be taken to Germany for adoption. Svetlana knew what trouble we were in. I never saw my sister or anyone ever so terrified. Only as we drove away did Grandpa come out of the house to see what was going on.

When Grandma came home and Grandpa told her what had happened, she began to beat him with everything in the kitchen. Then she suddenly went outside and began to run towards Mozor. She knew she had little time, so she ran the whole way in her long skirt, saying to herself, "What can I tell Maria when she comes home? What will I tell her? That I didn't save her children? Oh my God, what will I tell her? I cannot tell her I did not save her children." She also swore at her husband, swore to kill him if she did not get the children back.

She somehow made it to Mozor, where her daughter, Vera, lived. Vera was my mother's sister; she was very beautiful but she had married a painter who had a hunch back and red hair. I had listened many times to my sister Svetlana imitating Grandma's constant prayers about Vera: "Dear God, why did she marry a red-headed hunch back?"

She went directly to Vera's house and told her we were in the Mozor Camp. The two of them then went in to tell Vera's husband, Ivan, who was in the process of painting family portraits from photos the German commandant had given him. The two women explained what had happened, fell to their knees, and begged him to ask the commandant to spare us. But Ivan's mother, who lived with them, said, "No, he won't go. It is very dangerous."

But Ivan spoke up and said simply, "No, mother. I will go." And he left the house immediately.

At the camp, he was escorted in to see the commandant. Ivan had never met Svetlana or me, had never even seen photos of us, but he couldn't admit this to the commandant if he were pleading for our lives. So he just said he'd like to pick up two children who were his nieces. The commandant agreed immediately. Over the camp intercom, he told his soldiers to assemble the children taken yesterday from nearby villages. Then the commandant gave Ivan his own car and some soldiers and sent him to our barracks. Ivan was worried during the whole ride that he would save the wrong children.

Svetlana and I and about thirty other children were sitting on benches when the door swung open and a man came in. Svetlana saw his red hair and his hunch back, and wondered if this was the man her Grandma prayed about so much. But how could he be here with German soldiers? Then she ran up to him and threw her arms around him and said, "Vera's husband, Vera's husband." She didn't know his name. But he embraced her warmly, and they collected me; we left right away in the commandant's car. On the ride back to Vera's house, Ivan whispered to my sister, "You are Svetlana, aren't you? And this is Lilia?" Svetlana assured him yes.

8

As soon as we entered Vera's house, Grandma took us away, and we started walking back to our village. It was early spring, so no leaves were yet on the trees, just buds. Grandma was crying. She'd carry me for a while, then put me down and cry some more, then carry me a little more and then start crying again and put me down to walk a little. I was weak, but in this way we made it home late at night and went into the house.

We could hear Grandma in the kitchen throwing things at Grandpa, yelling at him for not saving the children for Maria and hitting him with a pot. Then she gathered some things and packed us all into the cart. Grandpa guided the horse into the forest to hide us better. After a few hours, we stopped behind some trees. Grandpa got out and went ahead to look. He came rushing back and quickly drove the cart ahead. We heard him tell Grandma, "We can't stay here. They are all dead." We went deeper into the forest and that morning arrived at a little house. We stayed there with some relatives until word came that the Germans had packed up and left. We cautiously moved back to Urovichy, not quite believing the Germans were gone for good.

Not long afterwards, my father passed through Grandma's little town one night and took Svetlana away with him for schooling while he continued to fight in the army. I awoke and found myself alone without knowing why. I was very upset. Since the Germans seemed to be gone, Grandma quietly moved me into a little room next to the oven. I lost my speech completely without Svetlana. I never spoke or answered a single question and seemed to have diarrhea all the time. Grandma was very worried about me, but the fighting and bombing was still so close. What could she do?

My mother and brother fought with the Byelorussian partisans, my mother as a nurse and my brother Anatoly as a spy. Because he looked like an ordinary Byelorussian little boy, Anatoly was assigned to go into German-occupied villages and find out how many Germans were there, if there were any tanks or large guns, and if villagers knew of any plans for German missions in the area. But when mother developed heart problems they were both sent to Moscow. The Byelorussian partisans had grown famous, since about one in four Byelorussians was killed in the war. They were given special recognition and honors in Moscow, so mother was able to get some money due her and my father, even though her papers had been burned. She was assigned to an orphanage for children from Leningrad. Near the end of the war she asked for some American Care packages with warm clothes and a few nice dresses for Svetlana and me. She packed them and got on a train with my brother to come find me. There was still much bombing during her journey, and part of her luggage was destroyed. But she made it back to Grandma's village.

She came into my room and shook me until I woke up. "Lilia, Lilia, it's your mom. I am back. Lilia, it's your mom." I shook my head no, but said nothing. She sat me on her lap and tried to talk to me. I would not speak or show any expression, though my mother asked me many questions. She told me that in the Resistance camps when things looked the worst, she and my brother Tolya would tell the story of how, on the night they left to join the Resistance, I fell from the oven right into grandpa's vodka, and how this made them laugh and laugh, sometimes till the tears came. I showed no expression. Mother cried that the war had made me deaf and mute; she had a heart attack that night. There was no doctor to help her, just Grandma with a brew of special tea. They laid her down in the bedroom. I could see her through the open door, but I did not speak.

Anatoly stayed with me and played with me all the time. He washed me and fed me, and kicked a ball with me, but still I did not speak. A few days later, he teased me with a big round brown thing, making motions he was going to eat it. I rushed him—"It's mine, it's mine!"—and scratched and tore at him until he let me have the thing. He ran into mother's bedroom, and told her I had spoken. She got right up and came to me. I said, "It's mine," and took my first bite ever of a cookie. Immediately I spit it out. I had never tasted anything sweet before so I didn't like it.

My mother asked me if I knew who she was. "NO," I said. She asked me lots of times over the next few days, but I always said, "NO." When she insisted she was my mother, I said, "No, my mother is in Moscow, and my father is killing fascists." She could not convince me otherwise.

She gave me the American dresses she had brought with her, soft colorful dresses with flowers and bows. One in particular was brightly colored, with brown, gold, and green sequins streaming down from neck to hem, like a peacock. The sight of this wonderful, sparkly dress shocked and stunned me. I had never seen anything so beautiful. I put it on, and my mother gave me black shoes with a strap, and socks with two little bows above the ankle.

That night she sang me a sad but nice ballad, "As I left you, your white dress shone like the moon, and you waved to me with the white veil from your head." Mom explained that she had been singing this song on an outdoor stage in the middle of the war, when suddenly she spotted my father riding towards her on a military horse. He recognized her from a great distance. They were together for one day; then they had to part in opposite directions.

Mother received a note with my father's address, so she wrote him that we were all still alive. The next day he arrived by train with Svetlana, and we all went back to his village together. Our family was very lucky that not one of us was killed during the war. We were able to start out again as a family, though without family things. There was a lot of angry yelling between my mother and father about what to do next.

My father was appointed commissar, expected to talk to the soldiers about what they were fighting for. Everyone was supposed to fight "for our country, for Stalin." My father only said, "Fight for Russia" and never mentioned Stalin's name. My mother told him not to talk like this for fear someone would hear.

My mother and I went back to Mozor to visit Aunt Vera. She told us that Ivan, her husband, had been accused by the townspeople of collaborating with the Germans because he had painted pictures for the commandant. He was arrested and imprisoned temporarily in Mozor, but he was so frail and sickly that he died of a heart attack before being shipped to Siberia. Vera took us to the attic and showed us some small paintings she had hidden, depicting the commandant's wife and two little girls. My mother said the two little girls looked like they were about the same ages as Svetlana and me.

Even though Vera's husband had died, Vera was taking care of his mother. Vera had some nursing training and took good care of this bitter old woman. But they didn't speak much to each other. Vera could not forgive her mother-in-law for refusing to allow her son to try to save us.

I was not used to having enough to eat, but after we settled down I ate everything I saw, no matter whose plate it was on. When I reached for something on Svetlana's plate, she always let me have it. But my brother would slap my fingers and tell me, "No. Don't touch my food." I decided I hated boys. If I did manage to get some scrap from the edge of his plate, he would go for my plate, and I had to lie down on my food to protect it. Occasionally my mother or father would give me things from their plates, but not often. My dad would just say, "Lilia, Lilia," and look at me sadly. He tried to slow me down, saying I'd kill myself if I ate so much. But my mother assured him I would not die from eating, that I would just be uncomfortable. And I was. Despite diarrhea and stomach aches, I continued to be greedy.

We had so little. My brother saw an old broken doll in someone's back yard and that night dug a hole under the fence and got it for me. We gave it wooden legs and cleaned it up, then decided to make it a coat. We cut a square of dark velour from the back of mother's only chair, then pushed the chair against the wall. It made a nice coat, but the doll was in danger if mother ever found it. So we dug a hole under the house and hid the doll in the "basement." One day my mother discovered the doll and the missing patch of cloth on her chair and cried for days when we told her what we'd done.

My mother told a lot of stories about what happened to her during the War. The Germans had Extermination Patrols, whose only job was to search for and destroy Resistance fighters. These Patrols would surround a forest they thought might have Resistance fighters, set fires all around the edge, and kill anyone trying to escape.

One time Mother and Tolya were in a forest hospital camp when the sound of trees burning brought everyone outside. The flames almost surrounded them. Suddenly a horse and wagon dashed up to Mother and Anatoly, and the Resistance fighter driving yelled, "Jump in!" Mother wanted to take the wounded, but the fighter insisted everyone else was lost anyway. Mother threw Anatoly into the wagon and covered him with her body. The fighter drove right through the flames to the river. They barely escaped. Everyone else was killed. Later, that same fighter died in Mother's arms in another hospital camp.

Mother spoke of the job Moscow gave her in an orphanage for children whose parents had died in the Siege of Leningrad. Because of her reputation, she was given enough food to feed these children, but the Tartars in that town were so poor and miserable that they threatened to steal the food. My mother was issued a gun to protect the orphanage and slept every night in the storeroom. She told many potential thieves she'd have to kill them if they tried to take the children's food. Knowing her reputation as a partisan, they believed her.

All the children called her "mother." One small young girl was also named Svetlana, about the same size as my sister, although starvation made her look several years older. When mother finally got permission to go look for me, this little girl pleaded, "Take me too. You are my mother." But Mother couldn't get the permissions she needed in time, so she didn't take little Svetlana with her. When my own sister Svetlana died in her forties, my mother poured out to me how much she has always regretted not being able to save this other Svetlana.

The Russian poetess Anna Akhmatova wrote achingly about these very children of the Leningrad Siege.

> *Knock at my door with your little fist.*
> *I open.*

I used to open my door for you.
But now I am far away from you
Behind a very high mountain,
Behind the dessert,
Behind the wind and heat.
But I never betrayed you,
Though I didn't hear your last moaning.
You never asked bread from me.

Please bring for me a green little branch
Or a little green grass,
As you used to bring it to me last spring.
Please don't forget to bring a handful of water
From our clean Neva River,
And I'll try to wash the blood
From your golden hair.

2

Being Hungry and Poor (1944)

Our family was together for only a few months when my father, Vladimir, was assigned to organize the school system in Dorovna, a city in Poland which had been partially destroyed during the German occupation; the Germans had abandoned the city months before. Parents in that city had not sent their children to school during the war for fear of the Germans, but now they were asking for some schooling for their children. Father left immediately with Svetlana and Anatoly; Mother and I stayed with Grandma in Urovichy until he could find us a place to live.

It was spring, and Grandma was eager to celebrate this Easter. On Holy Saturday, she cleaned the whole house and invited several friends to share some of her Easter kissiel pudding. On Easter morning, she added beet juice to the kissiel to give it a joyful color, prepared six separate plates of it, and covered each one with a white linen cloth. She cooked some potatoes, cut up some cucumbers, placed them in the center of the table, and went outside to check her garden.

I wandered into the dining room and saw the wonderful table. I lifted up one of the linens and found the beautiful pink kissiel. I slowly scooped up a handful and ate it. It was so warm and tasty that I ate the rest of it; I then put the linen back over the plate and went on to the next one. I ate that too and covered the plate with the white linen just as Grandma had left it.

I couldn't stop.

When I had eaten all the kissiel, I wiped my mouth and hands, went into the kitchen, climbed up to the top shelf over the stove and hid myself.

Grandma's friends soon arrived. They drank some of Grandpa's vodka, sang, laughed, and danced. Then they went to the table and sat down. I watched from my spying place as Grandma said a prayer and the guests removed the linens.

There was a long silence. Grandma was speechless. Grandma never beat us children. She said it was a sin to beat a child. Nevertheless, she gave me a beating that night, and I went to bed sore. The next morning at breakfast I told her that it was a sin to beat a child. She was speechless again.

Father was having difficulty getting living quarters in Dorovna since the war had not yet ended there, but Mother decided we'd join him anyway. All five of us had to live in a tiny storage room in Father's school. Mother was very upset. "Why did you agree to take this job when you had no apartment, no place to cook, no place to wash? It's impossible!" There was a lot of tension for the family and a lot of bombing. Many nights we had to rush outside when the bombing began and hide in the trenches around the school.

Things improved when Mother got a job at the local Communist Committee Headquarters, cooking and serving during the day, typing in the evening. She was given a little house nearby for our family.

The first day of work, she and I walked the short distance to the Headquarters, a big mansion surrounded by a high stone wall. A policeman let us through a rusty iron gate. Mother told me the building used to belong to a Polish Count.

While Mom cooked and served breakfast to the officials, I sat quietly, looking around. The rooms were so big, filled with mouth-watering smells. A smiling man gave me a biscuit and some hot tea. When Mom came over, he joked with her about the bravery of partisans. He took us outside and showed us a huge swimming pool made of marble shaped like waves. My mother smiled and laughed back--then pushed me into the swimming pool.

The water was shakingly cold, but I was so frightened and angry at her that I started to swim around. I swam for a long time and wouldn't get out even when she called me again and again.

The next day, Mom called for Svetlana and me to come to the mansion and take home some leftovers. Normally the workers couldn't take any food, even if it was to be thrown out. But the smiling man greeted us. "I told the policeman at the door that Maria Filipovna can take food for her children and that you girls can come for a pot of hot tea whenever you wish." I think he liked my mother. As he promised, we got lots of fresh bread, tomatoes, cheese and sometimes a little caviar. And I went there often to swim alone in the cold, pure water.

One summer day, before leaving for work, Mom prepared all our food for the day: a big loaf of black bread, five or six hard-boiled eggs, and a big salad of potatoes, carrots, cukes, and beets. We children awoke late and then ate everything for breakfast. After eating, we scoured the house for a kopek (cent) to buy a bottle of water with gas bubbles in it from the old Jewish man down the street who had a cart with a tent over it. Whatever kopek we could find that summer we'd rush off to buy and fight over this incredible water. It made us feel so wonderful and unusual.

And then we'd continue our search for whatever food we could find. One night mother got father laughing, throwing up her hands and complaining, "They want to eat all the time! I give up! I can't feed them any more." He asked us, "Okay kids, are you hungry?"

"YES!!!"

So he took a big black pot, filled it with water and wheatina, sprinkled little colored candies on the top, and put it on the stove. When it was done, we ate the whole thing, even though we weren't very hungry.

My father and I and much of the town occasionally went to the train station when Russians who had been taken prisoner in the War returned from Europe. They were treated like traitors for being captured. Most of them were sent by Stalin to the Siberian prison camps for twenty years. Men missing an arm, leg, or eye got off the train too; they were taken to the hospital for further treatment. We never saw anyone we knew get off those trains. My father was always quiet and angry as we walked home.

I regularly took our big teapot with a lid to the Headquarters so Mom could fill it with hot lemon tea and give me some leftovers. One day the man walking in front of me slipped on the ice just before the gate. I laughed as he got up and brushed off his coat. I heard, "Sonofabitch, that damn ice is slippery."

I was following him and slipped in the same place, and my teapot and lid went flying. I got up and brushed myself off and said enthusiastically, "Sonofabith, that damn ice is slippery," and went inside to see Mom. I did not see the man behind me who followed me in.

That evening Mom said to me that a high official had said to her, "That daughter of yours is a character. She slipped on the ice today and got up swearing. She is so small and funny I have been laughing all day long." Maria had responded, "She never swears. She hardly even talks. Maybe she heard it on the street, but I'll ask her tonight." So when Mom asked me why I had been swearing, I was surprised. "I don't know what you mean, Mom." I had only repeated what I had heard.

A few weeks later, my mother took me to work with her again. After breakfast, the smiling man from the Central Committee told her that several people had heard my father complaining that the Russian people should have more normal freedoms and had shouted, "Look how we live! Look how we all live, after suffering so much during the War!"

The smiling man was no longer smiling. "Maria Filipovna, I'm sorry, but your husband's views are so contrary to ours that you cannot work here any longer. I'm sorry, but the KGB will not allow it. In one week, your house will be given to another citizen."

We went straight home to tell my father. Mother was so angry at him and in despair. "Because you can't keep quiet, I've lost a good job, the children have lost their supply of extra food, and our family has lost its home." I was very angry at my father, too. That afternoon Mother sent me to live with my father's mother, who spoke only Polish.

After a few months I returned to the family. Mother was working in a little restaurant serving beer and salty potatoes. We lived in one tiny room in an apartment building, sharing kitchen and bathroom with the other residents. Mother quickly got a better job serving food in another restaurant and keeping the books.

In the room next to ours was a very kind, aristocratic Russian lady who spoke French most of the time. Well-educated and well-traveled, she had spent many years in Paris but was now 84 and seemed to be without resources. My father wanted to help her, but she would not accept anything from us. So he asked her to give Svetlana French lessons. Since I was speaking Polish around the house, he asked her to give me Russian lessons. My sister and I quickly grew to love this sweet, imaginative lady, who taught us languages so well and told so many stories. My father happily paid her for the lessons, sometimes with bread, and she was able to stay in the room next to ours.

Meanwhile, Tolya discovered soccer. Each day, as soon as Mom left for work, he'd grab me and head for the grassy field across town. We were both barefoot. I wore an old pair of his pants rolled up at the bottom and held high on my waist with a belt, and I had pulled on one of my dad's huge undershirts. Because of ticks and lice, mother had shaved all my hair off, except for a little in the front. Tolya made me walk on the other side of the street from him.

When we got to the soccer field, he plopped me on a bench, ran out and played and played. Even barefoot, he was pretty good. I sat watching and daydreaming but eventually grew bored and hungry. So I'd whine, "Tooolya, I'm huungry!!" He shook his fist and made such an angry face at me from the field, I'd shut up for a while. But before long, "Toooolya, I'm huuungry!!"

Pretty soon all the players on the field were shaking their fists at me, until a few ran off and stole some apples and plums, threw them on the ground in front of me, and ran back to their game. I ate this dirty fruit, but before long started whining again. "Tolya," they'd yell, "she's so ugly. How did she get so ugly? I never saw such an ugly little girl." I was skinny, with baggy pants, no hair, no shoes, and whining. "Yes, they are right," I agreed. "I am pretty ugly. So."

One afternoon, I asked Tolya if I could go swimming in the nearby river. He said, "Please! Yes! Go! Swim!" Then he was back to his soccer game and I went swimming. There were boys in the river. They swam over and asked, "What are you, anyway? Are you a boy?" I just made faces at them, the uglier the better, and swam away. One of them tried to catch me, so I told him about my older brother, the soccer player, and his friends who'd all come running if I yelled. So they left me alone. After that, I was always eager to come with Tolya to the soccer field because I got to go swimming.

But one day, my mother and four co-workers came to the river for a lunch break. Eventually my mother noticed someone swimming alone in the river. She stood up and tried to see better. She wasn't quite sure if it was me, and she couldn't quite believe what she was seeing. I ducked underwater and swam up river as far as I could, and got out. I ran to the soccer field. "Tolya, I think mother saw me in the river."

Tolya immediately left his game, and we ran home. He hid my wet clothes and found me other things to wear. Then we waited. And waited. I thought about the wonderful river water, and Tolya thought about soccer. Mother didn't come home until late, but the first thing she did was imply I had been swimming in the river. I denied it. She was suspicious and asked me several times, "Think a little, Leonila Vladimirovna. I think I saw you swimming alone in the river." But Tolya backed me up. He didn't want to be forbidden to go to the field.

He played soccer all day long and came home exhausted every night. But the next day after a little breakfast of a potato and a pickle, he would be off again to the soccer field. This was what he did after the war.

One morning, however, I awoke early to hear my father calling to mom that Anatoly was missing. She rushed to Anatoly's bed--it was empty. Like crazy people, Mother and Father rushed from the building and went off in different directions, looking along the street, between the houses, then back to our building again.

Suddenly father had an idea and hurried with Mother to Tolya's room. The wood floor by his bed was being repaired. My father jumped from the floor to the dirt four feet down. He fixed his hat, lit a match and started prowling. He found Anatoly asleep in a far corner under the house, so tired from soccer that when he fell out of bed and rolled off the floor, he just stayed asleep. My mother was upset to learn that soccer had tired him so much, but father was not. "At least he is doing <u>something</u>, Maria, and not hanging out with a gang of Bolsheviks. Let him play soccer."

A few days later, Tolya gashed his foot pretty badly. He had to stop playing for three days. My mother found him some old handmade straw boots. He wrapped tissue around his wound and put the boots on, and was back to playing soccer. My parents said, "He needs soccer shoes." They had no idea where to get such shoes and very little money. They discussed and discussed, then left the apartment building. When they came back, they had the shoes. I think it was the happiest day of my brother's life. He loved those shoes and always took good care of them.

I was always hungry. One evening a friend of my father was visiting us. My mother was telling him how hard it was to raise and feed three children, and this man said, "Maybe I will take one of the children. Maybe I will take Lilia and feed her properly." I jumped up and rushed to my room, found a basket, and began putting all my clothes and things into it.

I returned to the visitor within a few minutes and announced, "I'm ready."

My mother said, "No one could feed you properly. Now put away your things," and everyone laughed. I never liked this man when he came to our house after that, because he had tricked me, and it was unfair.

3

Starting School

Father had gotten the school ready for students again. He had fixed it up during the summer, and announced that all the children should come in the fall. The school looked very nice to me when my mother and I saw it that first day. It was clean and seemed very big to me. Inside the classroom, each desk had two seats, and the desk was covered on the sides and front down to the floor, like a little cave under the desk. I was the youngest of the fifteen or so children, ages six to ten, who started school that day; but I wasn't the shortest. None of us had ever been to school before, because of the War. We sat perfectly still because we didn't know what to expect. We watched the teacher and did everything she told us to do. She was young and very kind to us. She gave us each a notebook and a pencil.

After the first week, my teacher sent a note to my mother reporting that "Lilia is not appearing in school until the second or third period. Please attend to this."

I started to school as usual the next day. I came to the first zebra (crosswalk), and looked both ways. I spotted one of the few cars in town coming towards me. I watched it carefully until it passed me and I watched it go out of sight down the road. I looked around hoping I could cross the street, but I spotted another car. As I was watching it approach, my mother came up to me and asked what I was doing. I told her I was afraid of the cars, and she said, "But you have plenty of time to cross before they get here. Come with me." I was not too late that day, and the next day Mother helped me learn how to cross safely by myself.

I was eager to go to school because we got a little roll around noon. I took my roll and sat in the cave under my desk to eat it by myself, for fear someone would take it from me. After I ate this food, I was ready to go home, but the teacher wanted to do something else. So I got permission from her to go to the bathroom down the hall, and then I went home. I did this again the next day.

We spent the next morning writing the letter "Y" over and over again. For homework, the teacher told us to fill another page with "Y" letters. I asked to go to the bathroom and then went home. I thought again of those lines of "Y" we had written, how long it had taken us. So I wrote one large beautiful "Y" that covered the whole page. The next morning, the teacher put a big "X" across my homework. She wrote a big grade of "1" (one) on the page, the lowest grade you could get. I hated that "1."

After lunch she refused to let me go to the bathroom. I had some tea at lunch so I had to go badly. I ducked under my desk, squatted down and went on the floor. The teacher called my mother into the school and told her what I did. My mother asked me, "Why have you done this, Lilia?"

"I had to go, Mom, and she wouldn't let me use the bathroom."

Mom addressed the teacher. "Why didn't you let her go to the bathroom?"

"Because she doesn't come back to class. She goes home, and I don't see her again."

Mom addressed the teacher, "If you don't let a puppy go outside, she will pee on the floor." But then she saw my homework. Mother told me if I didn't learn how to write and read, the school wouldn't give me any food at noon. I hated that "1" all over again. After that day I stayed in class in the afternoon, and I practiced hard with the other kids.

A few months later, my mother got another note from my teacher, but she didn't say anything to me. The next morning I left the house for school. I stopped at a toomba, a wide, round column with notices posted on it, and a little roof over it. I struggled to figure out each word of a notice about a concert. When I understood, I read it aloud, firmly, and proudly: "On the first of the month, Anatolyevna is coming to town to perform..."

The next sign was more difficult, but I puzzled it out and then read it out loud too. "Next Friday there will be a Meeting on Patriotism. The

Central Communist Committee announces the names to be discussed: Sergei Goraschenko, Marina Ivanoff ..."

I was interrupted by my mother, "Lilia, what are you doing? You will be late for school again. Come with me." She grabbed my hand and led me off to school. My teacher told her that there had been a marked improvement in my reading recently, but that it would be better if I were not late.

Occasionally Mother would stop by the school around lunchtime to see me. Then she would go to the restaurant, where she kept the books. She came home late, so Tolya and Svetlana were in charge of me after school. One afternoon they gave me a permission coupon for some bread and sent me off to the store, but I lost the coupon or it was stolen.

When I came home, I was afraid they would beat me, so I went to the woman in the apartment next to ours. I hid in her room and listened through the wall to the family's conversation. After they had eaten supper and I was still not home, I heard my mother say she was quite worried and just wanted me home. So I went to our door where I was greeted with hugs and relief. "She is still alive. Thank God, she is still alive." I was not punished that time.

Another day, while mom was at work, Tolya, Svetlana and I were having tea. I finished mine first and reached for Tolya's, but I knocked the big pot of boiling hot tea all over my legs and burned them severely. Tolya and Svetlana lifted me up and put me in a big round metal barrel we used to store water. They poured cold water on me for an hour, then put me in bed.

When mom returned that evening, she came in to see me. I was moaning softly in my sleep, but she didn't do anything and went to work early the next morning. Svetlana got me dressed, and Tolya helped me put on my boots; we all went to school. When we got home, they could not get my boots off because they were stuck to my skin and I was bleeding. So they put me in bed with all my clothes and the boots still on. Mom came home and looked in and heard me moaning again and realized something was wrong. She pulled back the covers and saw me fully dressed with my boots still on. She got one boot off before she realized what happened. She beat Tolya and Svetlana a bit with a towel and then got me to the military hospital where they treated my legs; I have no scars. After that, Mother always looked at me each night, and said, "Thank God, she is still alive."

Mom usually went to the market on Sundays, and she started to take me with her to help carry the food for the whole week. The market was huge, with long rows of apples, potatoes, eggs, milk, and cheese. The vendors generally rode in on their horses.

When I saw these horses munching grass near the market, I immediately demanded that my Mom buy me one, yelling, "BUY ME THE HORSE, MOM! BUY HIM! PLEASE BUY ME A HORSE!" Mom angrily asked me to stop bothering everybody with my yelling. But I never stopped. I continued my high-pitched crying about the horse, about how wonderful my future life would be if I had a horse of my own. We went back home quickly that day.

Next Sunday, my Mom went to the market again. But she warned me, "Please, you can go with me, but forget about the horse. Don't ask me even once. A horse needs a big barn and a big field to live in and be happy. We live in a small apartment." Mom's arguments convinced me, so I promised her I wouldn't.

But when I saw the horses, the beautiful horses, I began my screaming and crying, "HORSE, HORSE, BUY, PLEASE, HORSE." My mother was quite frustrated. "This is too much. I'll never take you with me to the market again." The threat of never seeing my future horse was pretty scary; I stopped and kept silence, but only for a while. My mother continued to take me to the market because she hated going alone. Each time I promised to be good, but I always ended up yelling for a horse. I was only six and just couldn't understand why my parents would deprive me of such a beautiful pet.

One night, my father was appointed moderator for the Meeting on Patriotism I had read about on the toomba. My mother took me along with her rather than leaving me at home alone. We entered a long, crowded building. Mom went to the front row, and I sat on her lap. She warned me to sit quietly and not move around at all because this was the headquarters of the town's Communist Central Committee, and she did not want any trouble for our family.

The meeting began with a speech about "the great Stalin," and then lots of names were read out. The people at the meeting started talking about the names and the things they had said and done. I felt sure the people whose names were read out would all be punished, but I didn't understand why.

After many people had spoken, there was a pause, so my father stepped forward on the podium and asked if anyone else would like to "address the people." The word for "address the people" happened to be the same as the word for "give a performance." Reacting to the second meaning, I jumped off my mother's lap and somebody lifted me onto the stage.

I turned around to face the people and decided to sing a song I knew. I sang a few lines but then forgot the words, so I said, "No, no, I forget it. I'd better recite a poem for you, if you insist." I smiled at my father, but he was motionless. So I told a story I had heard from my grandmother, about a rabbit and a fox.

> *A little rabbit lived in a forest in his warm, tiny house. One day he was sitting at the window having tea, looking out at the snowy winter day, when suddenly he saw a little fox, shivering from the cold and quite unhappy. The kind little rabbit opened his door and said, "Hello little foxie, what's happened? Why are you here and not in your cozy little house?"*
>
> *"Hah! Cozy house! I don't have a cozy house anymore. I will die out here tonight."*
>
> *The little rabbit said, "Oh no, you're not going to die. Please come in with me. My house is small, but it's enough for us." The little fox put his*

tail down between his legs, and came into the house. He sat quietly in the corner and had a little tea.

In the morning, the little rabbit said, "Okay, foxie. I have to go to work now. I have to find a turnip. Leave the door unlocked for me. If you want to sleep, go ahead. I'll just put the turnip into the oven, and wake you when it's ready."

When the little rabbit came home from his job, carrying the big turnip in both arms, he pushed the door with his leg, but it did not open. He began to beat the turnip against the door, calling, "Please, little foxie, let me in. I'm frozen and hungry." But the door stayed tightly shut.

Suddenly the little fox opened the window and said, "What are you doing here? Such a noise you are making! You are disturbing me. Get out of here."

The rabbit was shocked and began to cry. He dropped the turnip, went away to his auntie's house and told her what had happened. But Auntie only shook her head, and said, "Oh my god. The forest has a little foxie. And the forest has a little, stupid rabbit."

When I finished the story, the people on stage looked down and covered their faces with their hands. The audience, however, burst into applause. My mother came up and grabbed me by the hand and pulled me down the main aisle and out of the building.

The meeting ended shortly afterwards; my father laughed all the way home. He was laughing so hard that he couldn't speak. When my mother tried to scold me, my father said, "Maria, stop it. Lilia's story was great. She sent them the message that we are all like this little rabbit who was so easily tricked and cast from his home."

The next day my Mom stopped in the middle of her cooking and said to me, "Oh my God, Lilia, how have I endured all the ordeals I've been through in my life. Not just me, but all our generation who were born before the Revolution. It's been starvation and war, prison and death, and more starvation. Just to survive has been difficult, and we still have nothing. How did we do it?" I didn't say anything, but I thought about how she had cared for the children in the orphanage at the end of the War, and I thought about how we got our orange cat.

It was late one night, and Mom was coming home from work in a downpour and heard a weak cry. She saw a scrawny orange kitty struggling out of a shallow puddle. Finding two sticks, she used them to lift up the kitty. She walked the rest of the way home holding the kitty in front of her on the two sticks. When she got home, she dropped the wet kitty on the floor and said to us, "Here. Take care of this." Then she went off to her room. We took the kitty into the kitchen and washed her in warm water, dried her off, and gave her milk from a spoon.

The kitty grew into a huge, fluffy orange cat. She was a great hunter. She used to catch mice and birds, sneak into my mom's room, and put them on her pillow. My mom closed the bedroom door at night, but when she turned the light on in the morning, she often found a gift. That cat was devoted to my mom.

We could always tell when it was about time for Mom to get home, because this cat would disappear from the house. At first she only waited outside on the porch, but eventually she went down to the main road about a mile away. She greeted my mom when she got off the bus late at night. Mom was actually relieved to see this cat and talked to her all the way home. She complained to the cat about her long day at work and told her about the hot tea she would have when she finally got home and had fed the children. The cat followed her or sometimes went out in front to lead the way. When they got home, the cat would get some leftover sausage, and Mom would talk a little more to her. She was my mother's guardian angel.

My mom never talked baby talk with this cat but addressed her as she would an adult acquaintance. She never took the cat on her lap or was affectionate with her; instead she greeted her almost formally and asked her how she was. My mother was like that with all the animals in our house:

she rescued them and took care of them but never babied them. She left that to us.

The cat's regular feeding time was in the morning, even before we children ate. While my mother cooked, sometimes pancakes and bacon or an omelet the size of a plate, the cat sat looking out the window. She seemed uninterested, but I saw her ears moving and her whiskers twitching at the smells and sounds from the stove. My mother would load some food on a dish and suddenly order the cat to come over to her. This large cat would fly to the food and once ran into my mother's legs and toppled her. We children would get our breakfast only after this cat was served.

Late one May night in 1945, we were suddenly jolted awake by the all-too-familiar sound of heavy artillery. We had no electricity then, so I ran for some matches in the kitchen. Mother stopped me: "No, Lilitchka, no candles. It's a bombing. The War continues. Grab something! Outside! Hide yourselves in the trench where we usually go!" I took my blanket, Svetlana took her pillow, and Tolya grabbed his soccer shoes. The corridor was chaos: everybody in the apartment was running, crying, yelling, gathering, and giving orders to the children. We all ran outside and hid in the foxholes dug years before by soldiers. The explosions continued, and everyone was afraid.

One old man decided to go back inside for his cigarettes. He crawled to the end of the trench and stood up and looked around. He suddenly turned back to all of us. "It's not bombs, you cowards, it's fireworks!"

We peeked out. Then, in the sky, appeared bursts of red and white light, flowers of sparks! Over the big, round loudspeakers atop poles around the Central Party Headquarters, there was electrical crackling, a loud siren, then a garbled announcement. "Comrades and citizens, today is a glorious day all over the world."

"What did he say? What does it mean?" the women asked.

The loudspeaker voice yelled, "IT'S THE END OF THE WAR! THE WAR IS OVER! THE WAR IS OVER!"

Nearby, troops were firing their weapons in celebration and setting off fireworks. The war was over. My mother said simply, "I don't believe it. I don't believe it. No."

We danced, cried and hugged long into the night. The children played, laughed, and ran everywhere, in and out of the trenches. Adults laughed and cried, prayed that the men from their families would make it back home. Tea and bread appeared. We children ate, we laughed, ran and played.

The next day Russian troops paraded through our town on the way home, on horseback and on foot, in tanks, with artillery guns--and lilacs.

It was lilac time. We children raced around to every house, even to the government garden, picked huge armfuls of the flowers, raced back to the parade and tossed them on the proud, dusty soldiers. A blond man with a bandage around his leg lifted me up onto his horse and I rode with him for a few minutes. I could see all the people waving and celebrating along the street. I looked up at the soldier's rough, happy face and touched the colored medals on his chest. He gave me such a smile! When he set me down again, I ran for more flowers. I was filled with awe and excitement.

4

Pioneer Camp, Piglet and Cow

I finished the first grade all right. I was already a head taller than the other children my age, quite skinny, full of energy, and ready for new summer adventures. Because the school was doing well, my father was given a little house next to the school. We moved right in with our few possessions. Mother was very, very happy about this, because she felt we were being given approval by the local communist officials, and because it was important for survival.

Since Mom was very busy with work and still had difficulty getting enough food, she decided to send Svetlana and me to the government-sponsored Pioneer camp for the summer. She had heard they had some food there and fed the children pretty well.

The camp was somewhere outside the city. We arrived at night in a severe thunderstorm with lightning and wind and heavy rain. The Pioneer leaders settled me in a tent with five girls my age and told us to lie down and go to sleep. I went to sleep, but suddenly the tent was blown apart and destroyed; we got soaked. I knew that Svetlana and the older girls were somewhere else in the camp, so I took my pillow and my blanket and ran to another bigger tent screaming, "Where are you, Svetlana? Svetlana?"

It was dark inside the tent. I began to look for Svetlana, pushing my wet pillow into the first girl's face and yelling, "Svetlana? Svetlana?" But it wasn't her. I went to every girl in the tent and hit each one with my wet pillow to wake her up. "Svetlana, is that you? Is that you?"

I was screaming, and they started screaming too. "There's no Svetlana in here, no one. Go away and let us sleep!" They pushed me back out in the storm. So I found another tent and went in.

I hit the girl in the first bed with my wet pillow. "Is it you, Svetlana?"

The girl said, "Oh my god, oh my god. Is there nowhere I can hide from you?" It was Svetlana! I jumped into her bed and put my wet pillow next to hers and told her what had happened. She said it would be okay for me to stay, that nobody would prohibit it because the storm had caused such a disaster. I was so glad I had found Svetlana and slept the rest of the night, dreaming about breakfast.

The next morning I got right up and rushed into the eating building. I sat down at the first table. But I was told we had to do special exercises before we ate and I was sent to the exercise field.

"One, two, three, four...hands up, hands down, sit on the ground, now stand up. One, two, three, four." I did all these exercises and then rushed back to the eating barracks. During the rest of my time at camp, I was always the first one to the door.

I ran to a table and started eating. I was the first to finish my breakfast, so I was the first to ask for extras. Sometimes they gave me more porridge or maybe an egg or a piece of bread. But I always asked for extras.

After breakfast, we spent several hours learning songs about Lenin and Stalin, and reading verses about them, the only two topics at Pioneer camp. "Line up in rows and we will march and sing to the great Stalin." So we made rows and marched back and forth, and sang about how great this man Stalin was. Back and forth, singing, for hours.

They let some of us swim a little and read from the library. I often grabbed a book and ran somewhere under a bush to read, because so many kids teased me and made fun of me. The older kids threatened me, pinched me, or beat on me. Svetlana protected me sometimes, but she was a girl, so she couldn't do too much. She had her own interests.

I had one pretty good friend at camp. She and I used to sit on the wooden exercise gym put out for the children each day. Since the campers didn't exercise here, we sat on it and talked and played together there. If somebody chased us, we ran away. But we usually came back to sit on this wood again.

After the first week, I was pretty bored, actually very bored. Sometimes, at night we had a big bonfire, which was new to me. But we just sat around it singing the songs we had studied during the day about Stalin and Lenin and about our country.

We were taught special songs about how happy our childhood is in Russia, about how happy we are, the happiest in the world, how rich and prosperous our country is, how we are free and independent, and how our government takes care of us, how Stalin takes care of us, how Lenin takes care of us, even though he had died.

> *"We are Pioneers; we are the children of hard-working comrades"*
> *"Stalin and Mao, looking out for you, attending to you, watching out for you. Stalin and Mao, looking out for you. Stalin and Mao, looking out for you."*
> *"April is bright and full of flowers, the month when Lenin was born. January is wintry and cold, the month when Lenin died."*

The teenage Pioneer leaders taught us, "Lenin died; nevertheless, he is thinking about you. He is still with you." I was puzzled. I had never seen this Lenin before, so I didn't admire him; I couldn't even like him. But the leaders said that he had died and is still thinking about me. "Oh, my god, he is a ghost." This was my perception.

After a few weeks, Mom visited us. She asked me how I was doing there. I said, "Okay. It's pretty good here. There is enough food, and I am going to get married."

"What???"

I repeated, "I am going to get married. I have a fiancé here."

She said, "Okay, Lilia, bring me your fiancé."

I ran and called our Pioneer leader. He was a big boy, about sixteen, who never paid any attention to me. But I wanted to marry him because he wore a red scarf. I told him, "My mom wants to see you. You must follow me."

I led him back to my mother, who made a very angry face at him and said, "What does it mean?"

He stuttered but didn't say anything. At sixteen he was already afraid of questioning and didn't understand what the problem was. My mom saw that he was frightened and embarrassed, and she shouted more angrily, "What does it mean?"

He said, "I don't know, I don't know what you are asking me about."

"What does it mean? Who let you get married? Who let you even talk about marriage? What are you going to do?"

He looked at her, and at me, at her, and almost fainted. My mom didn't say anything else. She just grabbed me by my collar and went to find Svetlana. Then we left.

Mom took us home from Pioneer camp. She discovered a rash on Svetlana's hand, along with redness and swelling of her fingers. My mother told us Svetlana had caught an infectious disease, probably from shaking hands with other Pioneers.

Mom spent a lot of time treating Svetlana's hand. She found lice in our hair, too, so she cut it all off and rubbed a special ointment into our scalp. This ointment had some very strong chemical in it that made her gold ring black. I was afraid my head would turn black, too, and maybe even my hair when it grew back. Despite my fears, she applied this strong compound to our heads several times each day.

I remember my mother's worrying while she treated us, "Oh my god, I decided to save time by sending them to this Pioneer camp. But in reality it turned into big trouble." She spent the whole summer treating Svetlana's hand and our lice and then diarrhea. Neither Stalin nor Lenin came to take care of us.

* * *

In 1946, I started the second grade.

One day, the first-grade teacher did not show up for class, and no substitute teachers were available. So my father, as head administrator, came into our school and picked out a fifth-grade boy to teach the first grade. He showed him the reading lesson for the day and sent him into the classroom. This boy came out of the classroom after only a few minutes and said, "I'm not going to teach them. I'd better go to my math class." And off he went.

My father said, "Okay, fine. It's okay. I'll get another teacher." So he came to the second-grade classroom and asked me to come out into the hall.

He said, "Lilia, today you are the first-grade teacher. You are going to teach today's reading lesson. You are a good reader. So first have the children read from this chapter in their books, chapter twelve. Give each child a sentence to read, like 'The pig was sleeping in the mud.' And then ask them about the sentence, 'Where was the pig sleeping?' Then go to the next sentence and the next child. When you are finished, ask some more questions about the story and what happened to the animals. Keep them busy and attentive to you, okay?"

I said only, "Yes," took the reading book from my father, and marched down the hall to the first-grade classroom. The children seemed quite small to me, perhaps because I was tall for my age. I went right in and walked to the front of the classroom, very serious and formal. I turned to the students.

"Open your books to the story for today. I am your teacher."

A little girl pointed her finger at me and said, "I know you. You're Lilia. You're not a teacher."

I announced that I was not a Lilia, that I was the teacher. Then I pointed to a boy in the first row and said, "You read the first sentence."

He said, "No. I won't."

I walked the few steps to his desk and put my fist in front of his nose and said formally, like a teacher, "You must read the first sentence, or else you will be made to go stand in the corner." I pointed to the corner in the back of the room. I returned to my place in front of the teacher's desk. "Now, read the first sentence."

He read the first sentence, and I asked him a question about it. I liked the story, so I decided to assign parts to everybody. "You will be the fox, and you will be the tree, and you will be the wind and make a sound like this..." I illustrated what the wind sounds like, and the little girl made the sound of the wind during the whole story. We read it sentence by sentence, with each student reading the part I had assigned. I asked a question about the sentence after it was read. My father was out in the hall looking through the glass door, but I pretended not to see him since I was the teacher. Soon the bell sounded, and we finished up the story. Then everyone took a break. I closed my book with a bang and marched out of the classroom as though a drummer were playing.

My father said that the next class was math, and he showed me what drills to go over, again instructing me to ask the children questions and have them give the answers. After the fifteen-minute break, I marched back in and announced that I was the math teacher. This class went okay, and the last class was just homework, so all I did was walk up and down the aisles watching the children. I loved being the teacher and asked if I could do it again.

At supper that night, my father told me I was "something special, something very special." He said to my mother that I was a very good first-grade teacher. The first-grade teacher was back the next day, but she had a sickness; so I got some other chances from my father to teach that year.

During the second-grade school year, I arrived home after school one day and saw that our front door had been broken. When the rest of the family came home, my father told us we had been robbed. All the winter clothes had been taken, all the silverware and plates, and the clothes from America, Mother's jewelry, her ring and bracelet and beautiful coat, even the little money she had hidden in the kitchen. We had nothing again and had to start all over.

Later on, at the end of March, I was coming home from my long, dull, boring music lesson, happy to have escaped it and to be walking home as a free seven-year-old. Suddenly, just inside an open window, I saw a huge, fluffy, shiny black cat, sleeping on his side on a soft pillow atop a little stool, with his paws bent over his fat belly. I could not resist him. I reached through the bars in the window and grasped this cat's neck fur, yanked him out the window and put him inside my jacket. Squeezing him tightly, I ran down the street.

I had dreamed about just such a cat: fat, with short paws and shiny black fur. I wanted him for my own, because my brother and sister and I were always fighting over our two cats, arguing about who owned them and whose lap they would sit on. But now I had my own cat.

The owner saw me and came out of his house to chase me, so I ran and ran as fast as I could. Going around the corner of my street, I slipped on the ice, and the cat said "fzzzzshhhht" at me and escaped from my grasp. I got up quickly and ducked inside our house, hiding behind the door in the bedroom.

Through the crack, I could see my brother sitting in the living room wondering what was going on. Suddenly the door opened and the big owner came in and shouted, "Where is this little robber? I saw a girl with a green coat come in here. Where is she?"

My brother said, "There is no such girl here. I live alone with my parents. What's the matter?"

The big man replied, "She has stolen my black cat, and she ran into this house. I'm sure my cat is here."

My brother bent down and reached under his chair and pulled out our black-and-white cat and held him up to the man. "Is this your cat?"

"No, mine is all black."

My brother said, "I have another cat." He got up and came into the bedroom, punching me with his fist as he came through the doorway. He reached under the bed with one hand, pulled out our huge orange cat, and went back to the living room. He held it up and asked, "Is this your cat?"

"No!"

"Well, that's all the cats we have here."

The man headed for the door and said, "No. I have to go find my cat." He slammed the door behind him.

Svetlana had been in the kitchen. When she and Tolya were sure that the man had left the yard, they fell down and laughed, kicked me, and threatened to send me to prison. I pleaded with them not to. Then Tolya said, "Listen, Big Eyes, we've told you a thousand times that you cannot take whatever you see. You know what will happen when we tell Mom and Dad." I screamed and yelled for them not to tell what happened. They told me I had better not go to school tomorrow but hide under the bed all day.

For the rest of the school year they tortured me about this shiny black cat with the soft belly that I tried to steal. Whenever we were eating without my parents, they would suddenly look out the window and take a deep breath, shouting, "There he is. There's the man looking for his cat." And I would rush to hide under my bed, and they would eat the rest of my dinner. I believed them every time, but I never saw this cat's owner, and he never returned to our house.

My sister, brother, and I continued to fight over our two cats even after I tried to get us a third one. A few months later, at breakfast, they told Mom and Dad about my attempts to get a third cat. Later that day, someone in the neighborhood called my mother to come and take a kitten from her new litter. So Mom went and brought home a little kitty, and Svetlana and Tolya and I started to fight over who would hold the kitty and who would sleep with it. Finally our parents sent us all to bed, and we took the kitty and piled into one bed and fell asleep.

In the morning when we got up we couldn't find the kitty and started blaming each other and looking around. Our parents came in to see what was going on, and made us get out of the bed. Mom pulled back the covers, and there was the poor kitty, but not alive. My mother lifted her and held her up. The kitty was so flat that my mother started to laugh and could not stop. Svetlana and I were so sad that the kitty had died in such a way, but my father couldn't help laughing too.

But a few moments later he got angry and told us, "That's it. I've had enough. From now on, there will be no more kitties, no more cats, no more dogs, nothing else alive in this house." He put his hands on his face and shook his head back and forth. "I don't know, Maria," he said to my mother, "I don't know. They are so stupid. Maybe they are underdeveloped because of the War and being under the shed for so long." He turned to us on the couch, and decided, "From now on, instead of playing with cats, you will read books. Yes. Go right now into the library and find a book, all of you. Go on, get going."

So we went to my father's library room and I happened to pick Emile Zola's *Germinale* about miners, about erotica and love in the French style. This was my first adult book. I began sounding out the words aloud while following with my finger: "He...put...her...on...the... pillow...and...tore...off...her...clothes...and..." My father grabbed the book away from me and began laughing, "Not that book, Lilia. You need children's tales." He gave me a book and I began to read. The stories were very good. It was the start of my hunger to read.

Later that day we buried the kitten and put a little cross on the grave. I cried a little but finally subsided. We did not add more live pets to our home for several months after this flat kitty. We eventually got another dog named Trezor.

Whenever my little friends and I started to play outside, somebody would come along and interrupt us. They would tease us or make fun of us, or steal our little belongings. So we were desperately looking for some quiet place to play. We were walking on the sidewalk, when suddenly we came to a large metal box, with steps leading up to it, and a fence around it. It was about two meters tall and about a meter wide. The gate was open, so we went inside and found a wonderful clean space, with a brick wall at the end. We played here, put our dolls around and played peacefully. Then we took all our stuff home, but the next day we went there again and began to play.

Suddenly we heard a man saying, "Girls, girls, O my god, what are you doing in here?" He was a large man carrying a lot of tools in his belt and pockets. Standing inside the box with us, he said, "You know girls, this area is strictly forbidden to play in, because this is a high voltage box. If you touch it, you could be killed. There was a big lock on it, see? How did you get inside?"

We told him the lock was open and that we had played there yesterday, but we had not touched the metal box. He said, "Girls, girls! Get out of here immediately! It's very dangerous to play here. It's a forbidden area and no one should be in here without special equipment." He opened the gate and helped us get our toys out, and together we left.

When school ended and the kids were no longer around, my parents decided to raise a few animals in the schoolyard. Before my mom went off to work each morning, she would always remind me to feed our piglet. This pink piglet began to follow me around everywhere, just like a dog. The people in town started calling me, "the girl with the piglet." I really didn't like being seen with her, and she used to make me angry. If she followed after me, I would run back to her and yell at her to go away, but she would just hide under a bush where I could hear her breathing. Then when I went on my way again, she would rush out and follow me, happy as could be.

Whenever this pig was hungry, she would squeak and complain in a high-pitched, short whine. If she was not fed right away, she would whine louder and longer. I wondered how long she would complain, so one day I didn't feed her right away. My mother came home and heard the whining, and asked me, "Lilia, have you fed the pig?" I shook my head no. "Why not?"

"I am listening to see when she will stop whining. It's a scientific experiment." That pig would whine all afternoon if she did not get her food.

One rainy day my mother came home with a cow, which she added to the schoolyard. She spent time training it not to give a long "moooooo," for fear of disturbing the neighbors. After the training, this cow would only give a short little "moop" and stop.

The cow quickly ate all the grass in the schoolyard. My mother gave me the job of taking the cow into the countryside for feeding, so that we could have fresh milk. I usually slept late during the summer, but when it was time to go, the cow started giving out a series of short little moops until I had to get up. I went right to the schoolyard and put my fist on her big wet black nose and said, "I'm going to kill you if you don't shut up." I called her all the swear words I knew, but nobody heard me.

I found it boring at the fields, watching cows eat grass. So the next day I took the cow through our city, across streets and through the traffic lights to the other side of town where there was a swimming lake. My mother had made me take the piglet too, because the neighbors complained that the piglet whined all day when she was alone. The piglet and I spent all day swimming and the cow ate what little grass she could find in the sand near the lake. That night she did not give much milk, and she didn't give much milk after that either, because I returned again and again to that lake.

I loved swimming and being in the cool water, and after a while, even the cow would get in the water. She would dunk her head in the water up to her ears, and seemed to find a few things to eat under there. The piglet ate mussels and everything she could find. The cow had a few mussels too sometimes, but I think mostly she ate sand.

We had to pass a prison on the way to the lake, and they had some very green grass in the front and around the walls. I called up to the guard in the tower about my cow. He yelled back, "Sure, you can leave her here. I'll tell the next shift that you'll be back this afternoon." So finally the cow had a good meal or two, and gave a lot of milk that night and the next morning. The guards minded my cow often after that, except on days when the guards said the warden was coming.

I was still embarrassed walking home from the lake through the town streets with a cow and a pig following me. I was trying to be an independent eight-year-old, so I often hurried ahead. But the cow would speed up too, and start moop-mooping, with the pig right behind her. I thought that the cow wouldn't follow me so closely if she weren't so hungry, so I took her to the clover fields, which was strictly forbidden. I hid behind the bushes and the cow rushed for the clover, gulping down the greenery because she knew I would quickly come get her and leave. She always had clover hanging out of her mouth when we started back through the city. My mother was quite pleased with the milk she gave that night, so I tried to stop there every once in a while, but mostly the cow ate sand at the lake.

When the cow wouldn't give milk, Mom would feed her at home. Mom used to wonder aloud how it was possible for that cow to eat all day in the fields and eat more each night, and still only give a glass or two of milk. I guess you can't make much milk from sand.

There were tons of movies brought back to our town from Germany by the Russian soldiers after the War. They were mostly American movies, with famous stars like Greta Garbo and Marlene Dietrich and Dina Durkin. All the movie houses in our town were open and busy, and movies were cheap to see.

One day, with the cow following me, I came upon the theater for the first time. Because it was so hot, the back doors to the theater were wide open and I could hear the film. I told the cow to stay still by the open door and not to move from this spot. I threatened her with my fist held against her black nose. Then I crawled through the door and under the nearest seat, which was in the front row. I saw the rest of the show, at least the bottom half of it, and then crawled back out at the end, and the cow and I continued toward the lake for a swim.

The next day I sneaked into the theater again, but I fell asleep under the seat and didn't wake until the audience was applauding at the end. I decided that I wasn't going to stay under the seat anymore.

Saturday afternoon was the best day at the movies, so on that day I crawled around until I found an empty seat and then I popped up and sat in the chair. By chance my brother and sister happened to be sitting right behind me. Tolya started to pound on me, demanding, "Where's the cow, you little idiot? Where's the cow?" I told him it was waiting for me outside the door, but he made me go out with the cow and I didn't get to see the movie. My cow was waiting for me, and we had a nice swim that day. But I was hooked on the movies.

When it got cooler and the theater doors were no longer open during the show, I often got into the theater lobby by saying I had to go to the bathroom. Then I crawled through the bathroom window into the theater. Sometimes I said my mother was in the theater and I needed to see her. I never had any money, so I never paid for the movie. And that cow always waited for me.

One day Mom went out to the fields herself to bring me some sausage and potatoes. But the people there said, "No, the girl with the pig never comes here anymore. Try the lake." Mom found us at the lake, and took the cow and the pig home, but I wouldn't come out of the water, not until she had left.

Decades later, after my sister had died, my mother quit smiling and laughing, except for one time that I can remember. I was lecturing my niece Tanya about being helpful, and I reminded her about how I myself had taken care of the family cow one summer. My mother overheard me and started to laugh and couldn't stop. She sat on the couch, and said to us, "You took care of the cow? You took care of the cow? O Lilia! How did I dare give that cow to you? I don't know. I have felt guilty about that poor cow all my life until this moment." She was laughing and crying for a good long time that day, remembering that poor cow.

5

Adventures

When I was about ten or eleven, I knew I was a tall and skinny girl, but I didn't care because I had so many projects I wanted to see and do. Each day I got up and wondered what I would find that day, or where I would venture. Even though I was almost a foot taller than my classmates, which was considered very ugly in Russian society at that time, they didn't tease me because I was not afraid to beat on them if they did.

Reading a book from my father's library started off as a punishment, but soon I began reading all kinds of books. And I got a lot of ideas. I read a book about explorers who made it to the North Pole, about the courage it took to try such a daring thing and succeed. I imagined myself arriving at the top of that snowy world when nobody thought it was possible. So I decided to go to the North Pole.

I organized eight of my friends and gave them a little speech. "We are going to do something brave and daring, something that will take secret preparation. We will go to the North Pole. We must begin by storing some food."

My friends had many ideas for the trip. Olga drew us a map heading north across the Tiagra and onto the tundra. Boris suggested we could ride the deer across the tundra. My friend Tanya said we would have to wait until winter froze the ocean before we could cross it and arrive at the North Pole. I told them we would kill a white bear there and burn the fat for light, and make heavy coats for everybody from the one big white fur skin.

We met regularly to plan our journey. Each of us began by stealing some flour from our homes. Some brought cans of food, too. We found a wooden box to hide it all in. I put the box in the old shed in our back yard, in a dark corner where no one would see it.

I knew from my reading that our supplies must be carried by sled. We were not sure where to find one, so Sergei drew a plan of how to build it using our box. Dasha figured out how to attach the sled to our basset hound, Trezor, so he could pull it for us.

We made a harness and tied it to the wooden food box. My friend Tanya found Trezor behind the shed. When the eight of us surrounded him carrying the harness, he lay down on his back and started howling. I don't know if he was afraid or just wanted us to scratch him, but he was howling. We stood him up and got the harness on him, and urged him to start pulling. But he just lay down again, and tried to wiggle out of the harness.

We kept trying to train him, but he never took one step to pull our food box. We decided he was a lazy dog, with no sense of generosity and no urge to do daring things. "And besides," I said, "he's not strong enough for a trip to the North Pole anyway. What about that big dog next door?"

This big dog was always barking at us, so we made a plan to get him familiar with us by feeding him through the fence. Then we would steal him and put him in the basement while we trained him. Each day we offered him food through the broken fence. Each day he ate it and then barked at us. We wondered how long it would take before we could get near enough to steal him and begin his training with our sled. We never considered giving up.

But one day we went into the back yard to feed this dog, and almost ran into my brother. He was standing with his foot on our North Pole expedition box from the shed.

"Hello, Lilia! This is your box, right?" He bent down and opened it. "You took this food for some reason and hid it in the shed. What are you planning?" He stood up and crossed his arms and stared at me. "I know you did this. Now tell me all about it."

We were all shocked that we had been discovered. "It's for our trip," I mumbled.

"What trip?" he demanded. So I told him about our plan to go to the North Pole. He began to laugh, and started choking and fell dramatically to the ground. He crawled to the house, and betrayed us to my mother.

She came outside. "Oh, no, my dear Lilitchka," she crooned. "The North Pole is far, far away." She put her hand on my shoulder as we all sat down on the ground. "Very few people have ever made it there. You can't go to the North Pole, my little ones. No child has ever made it to the North Pole. None has even tried. People die trying to get there. This is not a good idea."

My mother got a little upset. She shook her head back and forth, singing to herself, "Oh, no. Oh, my God. The North Pole? Oh, no, not the North Pole. Oh, my God." Finally she said calmly, "No, Lilia, you'd better give me this food. We'll use some of it for supper. You children go inside." She picked up the box and we silently trudged inside, with my brother taunting us and laughing. We enjoyed the blinney Mom made us from the flour. Although we had failed to set off for the North Pole, our hearts still wanted to try.

(A few years ago, when I finally escaped from Russia with my daughter Kristina, we landed in Iceland for a while on our way to America, and I saw a huge iceberg jutting up on the horizon. I wondered how far from the North Pole we were, and I was awestruck with the size and power of that iceberg. "No," I said to myself, finally giving up that old dream. "I don't think we would have made it.")

At some point during the summer, we were somewhere in another city, and the city was not too big. There was a swamp not far away, and in the middle of the swamp was a big island, with lots of trees and the ruins of a castle on it. Somehow, I was in the area, and spotted it myself. And when I saw the top of that castle, I said to myself, "Oh, my God. Look at that castle."

When I got home, I got into the yard and started to gather my friends again, telling them, "I saw a swamp, and in the swamp was an island with a castle on it. We must go explore it!" So we all started out for the swamp I had seen, and I vividly remember I was in front, and we went into the swamp, where the water at times came up to my waist, but never any higher.

We finally came to the island. When we got ashore, we walked through the trees and came to the ruins of the castle. It was overgrown with weeds and vines, with paths leading up to it, and some tunnels through the vines leading down to underneath. We were frightened by the dark tunnels and underbrush, and decided not to go further but to come back later.

[Many years later at the University, I found the book, *Children of the Underground*. And when I saw the book, I realized it was about this castle we had visited as children. The name of the city was the same, and the book described a forest, then a swamp, then this castle, but I don't remember the plot of the book. The story was not set in Russia, but in Polish territory. The book was written before the Revolution, maybe by Kokalevsky.]

During the next summer, after I turned nine, my Dad decided that his school needed some repairs. Pieces of the ceiling had been falling into the classrooms all year long, and the whole building needed cleaning and painting. He made an application for the money from the communist school committee. But he knew it would take at least a year to get it approved, so he borrowed the money himself and began the work. My mother scolded him for not getting the necessary papers and permissions beforehand from the Communist Party, but he didn't care.

He removed all of the desks from the classrooms and piled them up in the front yard of the school, and then worked on this project all during the summer. He began bringing books home from the school library, books of poetry mostly. He told us that Stalin had a policy that all these books should be burned, except the ones about Stalin and Lenin, and maybe Turgeniev because he only wrote about nature. My dad wanted us to read these books of poetry, and to learn all of them because it was possible all copies would be burned and nobody would know these poets and never see these verses. Dad brought home poetry books by Akhmatova, Blok, Svetaeva, Pushkin, and others, and I was reading and learning, reading and learning. And once he even brought me *Jeanne d'Arc.* It was dangerous to do such a thing.

I had started reading *Treasure Island.* I liked to be alone when I read so I could concentrate. One day, I climbed a tree to read a little more from this story, but I couldn't get comfortable. I climbed down and went next door to the schoolyard, and scrambled up to the top of the pile of desks. I got into one of the desks and started to read again. It was quiet and I had a nice view.

My sister Svetlana saw me from our kitchen. She came over and very quietly told me to climb down carefully, because the pile was not stable. I told her I was fine. When she added that she had something in the kitchen for me, I climbed right down and went home with her. She put a little butter on some bread and gave me two pickles, and I was happy. She sat down with me and said, "Little Lilia, I can't beat you anymore, you're getting too big. But you must be more careful." I was a lot of trouble, I think, but she was patient with me most of the time. She herself was always quiet and good and never ever got into trouble.

I hated doing my chores at home. My mother gave each of us twenty kopeks for some tea and a roll while we were in school, but I never bought anything. I just saved the money. It was 30 kopeks to see a movie, but I still sneaked into the theaters and never had to pay. When my brother Tolya wanted to go to the movies with some girls, he would be very sweet to me in the morning, calling me his little Lilitchka. Then I would be told I had to do the dishes or some other chore at home, which I hated, so I gave the money to my brother to do the dishes for me; but he always took the money and never washed the dishes. My sister Svetlana would always end up doing the dishes rather than see me punished. I would pay her too to do my other home chores, and she would do them.

Svetlana was the one who kept our apartment clean and neat; Svetlana was cooking the dinner, washing me, brushing my hair, fixing my curls every day, checking my class schedule, and just everything. Whenever she was at home, she was doing all these things, like a mother. It was normal in Russia, especially after the War, to take care of each other in the family; otherwise the family would never survive. Svetlana was the one who kept our home neat and clean. She managed to go to school as well as keeping our home clean and neat. The school had two sessions, and mine began at about 2pm, so I slept until noon; Svetlana finished the first session of the day, and came home at noon and woke me up, "Get up, get up. You have to go to school." She kept the whole place going. Besides cleaning and cooking, she planted tomatoes in the garden, and cherry trees. Anatoly and she found cherry trees somewhere, brought them home, and planted them. Anatoly and Svetlana did all the gardening; I never ever did any gardening, never even looked at it. It was not my kind of business.

I finished reading *Treasure Island* and was very impressed by it. I thought, "There is no island around here, not even any water. It's all very flat and dry. So where can I find a treasure? Where would people hide their treasure?"

I remembered that after the War, we had seen a lot of baggage left around the railroad station. I thought, "Maybe somebody buried a suitcase there, filled with jewels. Yes. I will look for treasure by the railroad station."

Our pig was big enough for me to sit on, so I rode him through the streets to the station, and found an old metal cooking spoon to dig with. I figured that people who bury treasure would not want to be noticed, so I went behind a fence to a spot not visible from the station and started to clear away a place to dig. The pig kept trying to root around my spot, so I tied him to the fence where he couldn't bother me. It was hot and sunny, but I kept digging all afternoon, sure that I would find a treasure. I rested at times next to the pig and then went right back to my digging. Finally I heard my spoon make a "Clink."

"I've found my treasure!" Thinking only of jewelry, I dug it out in a minute. It was still shiny even though it had been in the ground for a while. I clutched it to me and got back on that pig and said, "Quickly, get me home."

I sneaked inside the house past my brother, and hid the treasure under my bed. I was sure my brother would take it if he saw it, and I wanted those jewels for myself. I waited patiently until he left, then I got my dad's hammer and began trying to open the treasure. I banged and banged with that hammer. My Dad heard the noise from the school next door, and came over to see what was going on.

When he got to the door of my bedroom, he stopped. He gently told me, "Lilia, quietly set down my hammer," which I did. But I picked up my treasure and held it tight. "Give it to me," he insisted.

"But Dad, it's <u>my</u> treasure, not yours."

He yelled at me, "Lilia, it's not a treasure. It's a bomb, and it's dangerous. Give it to me right now!" I gave it to him because he was so serious. He carried it outside and across the street and put it down in the field. Then he went to the military base to report it. They told him dozens of children had set off such bombs and many had been killed. They came back with him to the field and got the bomb, and then they asked me where I had found it. I told them, and they went off to the railroad station. When they returned, they had three or four more bombs.

My father was really mad at me that night, and beat me with a towel. He told me I was not to go anywhere, not to touch anything. "Just sit in the house and do nothing for the rest of the summer!" I didn't leave the house for the next month, until school started. And my brother Tolya didn't let me forget it.

One day he would say, "Hello, sweet little sister. You're staying at home today? But it's such a nice day. We're all going swimming. Maybe we'll even look for a treasure." On the next day, he would say, "Hello, little bomber. May I see your treasures?" And he'd laugh and laugh. He had some new torture for me every day. I hated him. And my mother and father joined his side and teased me, too. I swore to myself that if I found another bomb, I would set it off against them. I also spent a lot of time thinking about where real treasure might be.

At the end of the summer, the Communist bureaucrats did not give their approval for the money for the school repairs, mostly because my Dad had done the repairs without getting their permission. They took away my Dad's appointment as district school commissioner, and we had to move immediately out of our house. Svetlana was very angry with our father. Mom had to sell the cow and the pig. We lived that long cold winter in a foundation in the ground, with no house on top, while my Dad paid the money back to the bank from my mother's salary. In the Spring my Dad got an appointment to teach in a school near Moscow. We moved into a little house near the school and settled in.

Just before my tenth birthday, my mother decided to take me to celebrate Easter in a small village further outside the city. Celebrating such holidays was not permitted in Russia generally, but people in small, distant villages were not watched by the police and KGB. Mom said there would be colored eggs, a special pie, and other little delicacies.

We rode the train all day and were welcomed that night in the home of Mom's friends. I got up very early the next morning to look around.

This village was atop a hill, and I could see another town on the hill across the river. I was curious, so I decided to go exploring. I started walking in a straight line towards my destination. In an hour, I had made great progress and came across a woman in a field. She stopped me to talk.

"I don't recognize you, my honey. You're not from around here. You came from the city for Easter, right? Where are you going?"

I told her, "I'm walking to that town over there. I want to look around and see what's going on there."

She immediately took my hand. "Oh, no. You can't go there. It's too far. The bridge is out, and there are only two trees to climb across. It is very dangerous, and you could fall into the muddy water. And you know, further on, there is another river with no bridge and then a swamp before you come to the town. You must go back home, little one. Who let you make such a trip?"

"No one," I told her.

She turned me gently around, away from the town in the distance, and I walked with her back to the house I had left earlier. "Just go inside, my dear, but don't tell anyone or they will beat you." No one was up yet, but they awoke soon enough.

My mother asked me right away, "Leonila Vladimirovna, why are you so dirty? You haven't gone somewhere, have you?" I mumbled something about going around the neighborhood, but Mother was skeptical. "Around the neighborhood... You've probably been half way around the city and back. Now go wash up before the celebration." I did, and we had a wonderful feast that day, with colored eggs, a tall brown pie speckled with dried cherries, some roasted pork, cold meat that shook like jello, and a warm compote made from dried apples, pears, plums and cherries. I didn't tell anyone about my attempt to visit the town, just as the lady had recommended.

After the celebration, on the train trip home, my mother recalled the time years ago that Dad had gone to see some of his relatives for Easter. His visit was noticed by people there, and a sarcastic article appeared in the local paper, noting that everyone else went to work each day, but Vladimir Rousak went to visit his relatives for Easter. "This is why your brother and sister and father did not come with us this time," Mom explained. "Pioneers and teachers should be at work." She had been afraid someone else would recognize my father if he came to the country and perhaps write something else in the newspaper.

About a year later, I took another trip. My brother was off somewhere at a sports camp for a week or so, and my mother and sister had left by train on the day before to visit my grandfather in Byelorussia. My father stayed home because he had to administer exams at the university where he taught.

I was outside by myself, just looking around, and I suddenly got very sad thinking that my mother had gone away on the train with Svetlana to see Grandad, and I was still at home. I decided, "I should go, too. Yes." So I put a big onion and a piece of bread in a scarf and tied it up. I put my little coat on, thinking that although it was warm now, it would be cool in the evenings and I would need it to keep warm on my journey. I looked at my dog. He was just sitting by the table looking back at me. I saw that he was a long dog, but with short legs. I figured he would be slow and get tired quickly on a journey, so I did not take him when I left the house.

I went to the train station. No one was around, and I stood between the steel tracks. My eyes followed the rails into the distance, and I started walking. Soon I was outside the city and was walking along on a fine day, when I again saw a woman working in the fields nearby. She put her hands to her mouth when she spotted me between the tracks and came immediately towards me. But I kept walking.

When she caught up with me, she asked where I was going, and I told her "Machanovichy." She said she knew of no town like that, and she swept the surrounding hills and country with her hand, saying "not around here."

I told her, "Of course not, auntie. It's in Byelorussia. My mom and sister have gone there to see Grandad, and I'm going to catch up to them soon."

The woman started ranting about children these days, how silly and stupid they were. "Don't you know it takes a train days to get there? You'll die if you try to walk there. Oh my god, go home, child. Turn around right now, and I'll walk with you, but you must go back to your home." She took my hand, and I let her lead me back.

When we reached the edge of the city where the roads started up again, she stopped and made me promise to go right home, but not to tell my father what I had done. "Do you know the way from here?" she asked. I told her I did, and she repeated her orders that I go home and not tell anyone where I had been. I did as she asked.

When I got home and opened the door, my dog jumped up on me and started barking. I grabbed him in my arms and my dad took our picture. I still have this picture. Then Dad saw the big onion and bread, and asked me about them.

"I was going for a walk."

Dad said to me, "Lilia, I want to talk to you now." He led me to his library, where I was only rarely permitted. "It's not easy to say certain things to you when your mother is at home." I recalled all the times my mother had reacted negatively whenever my father disagreed with anything political. She was always urging him to go along with things and not be noticed.

My father started by telling me that he had been administering history exams that day, and that he was particularly upset because the state examiners had visited his classroom. They complained that he had not mentioned Lenin enough. My father imitated the examiners in a queer high voice: "Why didn't you ask the students about Lenin, his date of birth, about the events of his life? There is no history of our country without Lenin. Why didn't you ask the students more questions about Lenin? It seems to us that there were not enough questions about Lenin."

My father stopped and quietly shook his head back and forth. He looked at me seriously. "Lilia, I do not know how, and you must not mention this to anyone, ever, but you must find a way to escape this country. You are young, so you must start to think about it now. Yes, think about how to get out of this terrible country."

Starting when I was about eight years old, my father had showed me books that told the truth about the 1917 Revolution in Russia. He told me that American soldiers had come to Archangelisk in the far northern region of Russia after the Revolution, and it was the real beginnings of a democratic way of living in Russia. The Americans rebuilt the bridges destroyed by the Bolsheviks; they rebuilt the railway stations, they built schools, they fed the population, and let the people elect their own mayors and officials. Some Russian workers traveled 200 kilometers to the area to get food from the Red Cross and American soldiers. But Stalin heard about it and made the Americans leave. All this I heard from my father when I was about eight.

After giving me the picture of me and my dog, he said he was going to tell me things because tomorrow he might end up in prison, and "if I didn't tell you the truth now, your little brain would be fooled by the Communist Party words." This is what he said, that he wanted me to know the truth that we are really slaves to the Communist Party. "You can never tell anyone about this conversation. Do you understand? No one, not ever. But you must always think about getting away from Russia and this Lenin. Remember." He was sure that I would never tell anybody, and it was true. I never did tell anybody what he told me. Not one word to anyone about politics.

By the time my mother and sister returned, my dad was without a job. My mother asked Dad what had happened, and even before he answered, she yelled at him, "I know what happened. Don't tell me. You could not teach Lenin. You could not mention Lenin. I know what happened. Why can't you mention Lenin? Why? Why? Why can't you teach about Lenin?"

"I can't," my father stated, and he turned away.

"Fine," said my mother. "You can't mention Lenin, and the children will starve." She gave up. "Fine." Soon we were kicked out of our official two-bedroom house, and had to rent one small narrow room for all of us. We slept on the floor. That winter, my father was taken away to prison, and Party members came and took all our clothes and furniture and even made me take off my coat and give it to them.

My mother knew a general from her days in the Resistance; with the general's influence, my mother was able to get my father off the train headed to Siberia and the work camps. He came back home within a few months.

I thought often about my father's words after he took that picture of me and my dog, urging me to do what I could to leave this god-forsaken land. I never spoke about this to anyone, not a single person, never--not to my brother, not to my sister, not to any of my classmates. I didn't want to be betrayed. Even later on as an adult, upon my return from business travel abroad, my colleagues and friends would ask me if I liked the foreign country. I always said, "No, only Russia."

After the war, I saw a lot of men in the streets who didn't have any legs, especially outside the hospital where they begged for money or food. My mother said that they had lost their legs in the War, and that either they didn't know where their families were or they were too ashamed to go home, so they stayed near the hospital. Some men had no eyes, some no arms. My father got put in charge of the home for blind people in the town. It was a government job, and we got a nice apartment to go along with his salary, so we were able to start over again. I used to visit my father at lunch time, because he could get me some food then. But he was seen and reported for giving me this food, so he lost that job too.

6

Lessons

I was attending the ballet school and the classes were wonderful. Our teacher was short and fat, Polish by origin, with a long, long bamboo stick, maybe three meters long. She could reach us from every corner. If we didn't turn our heads properly, if we didn't smile while making every move, even if we didn't have a proper look in general, she would get you with that stick. We had wonderful performances during our classes. I don't know if she beat me or not, but because of my "very good" performance, I can judge that she beat me quite a bit.

We enjoyed these ballet classes and were getting ready to put on stage Stravinsky's *Rite of Spring*. The day before our performance, our teacher suddenly announced, "Okay, you guys. I have allowed you to wear any costume you want in our classes. But to perform the Stravinsky ballet tomorrow, you must dress in a white t-shirt and a long dancing skirt, luminous and transparent, and to wear ballet shoes." I was puzzled, because no such skirt existed in Russia; there were just none of them. I was upset, thinking as I walked home, "She would like too much from us. What can I do?"

I got home after mom had gone to work, so I had a couple of hours. First, I made an outline contour of my feet and cut little pieces from Mom's linen napkins. I sewed them with a big needle; there, I had my ballet shoes. For a white t-shirt, I decided I would steal one from my brother and redo it for myself. I already knew how to do this. But the skirt was a real problem. I opened the wardrobe and looked thoroughly around. Nothing. Nothing at all suitable. I looked at the linen, but it was disgusting. It was a yellowish white, and far from translucent, sorry. I sat on the chair and stared out the window.

Suddenly, like a lightning bolt, I had an idea. I saw through the curtain. The curtain was translucent! I grabbed the big scissors, pulled over a big chair and climbed up on it. I cut off half the curtain, grabbed a needle and thread and started sewing. I made a wonderful luminous and translucent skirt from this. My final costume was really very good, by my standards.

But in the evening, my mom came home. She looked at the window, and asked, "Okay, why did you do that, Lilia?" I was upset because she did not ask Anatoly and she did not ask Svetlana. I thought, "Why did she ask just me?" I felt very humiliated that she asked only me. And she said, "I'm gonna kill you, just kill you for this."

I answered, "Okay, you are going to kill a very famous future ballerina."

"What?" She looked at me. "What did you say? A ballerina? You are going to be a ballerina? Look at yourself." She began to laugh. My brother was home, too, and he began to laugh. They laughed together in unison, and could not stop, so Mom forgot to beat me.

She started again, "Do you know that you will have to jump halfway across the stage?"

"I can do it right now," I said.

"I know, I know. You can do it right now. Okay, but that poor little male ballet dancer will still be on the stage. He can't carry you; you are twice as tall as he is." And they were laughing, getting so much pleasure from imagining me as a ballerina. Tolya was staggering around, acting out how my poor male partner would have to carry me. So I was not punished for destroying mom's curtain. She let me make my ballet costume, and go to the recital.

We danced to Stravinsky's *The Rite of Spring*. On our dance stage was a wire arch with flowers around it, and we stood on our toes and took short steps around this arch, with our hands above our heads, making new groupings. Mom was not there because it was not the custom for parents to attend these dance recitals, only the school children and teachers. We really danced well, almost professionally, it seemed to me. Everyone in our ballet class thought so; we were very proud of our performance.

***

That summer I went for an extended visit with my aunt and uncle at their country mansion near a lake. Uncle Anton taught biophysics at the Veterinary Institute. He had risen to the rank of major in WWII after leading his troops right into Germany; thus, he lived a secure life after the War. My Aunt Casimira was a successful gynecologist. Their mansion was a couple of hours outside Moscow, and they never had to leave it.

They had a big fluffy Siberian cat. Female cats in Russia are named Puska and males Vaska. This was Vaska, and he owned his own sofa in the sitting room. When he spread out on it with his long full tail, he reached from one end of the sofa to the other.

Dogs in Russia are given only a few names, too, either Jubbars or Trezor. Uncle Anton had a well-trained German shepherd named Jubbars. Since people were not allowed to carry guns in Russia, store owners hired big dogs as security guards. Jubbars worked every night in a big universal store and earned 600 rubles a month prowling the aisles of food and clothes. Only once did Jubbars catch someone; one morning the owners of the store found two young men sitting on top of a pile of boxes, with Jubbars down below, snarling and growling. The two robbers demanded, "Get that stupid dog out of here! Get him out of here."

Jubbars neither looked at me nor played with me except for one day when I was home all by myself. I got a little afraid when I heard Jubbars scratching at the door. I opened it, got down in front of him, and shook my finger at him, telling him sternly that I would let him in only if he didn't growl at the cat. He looked right at me, the only time he ever acknowledged me, so I let him in. He walked past the cat and into the kitchen, so I gave him some crackers and cheese as I had seen Uncle Anton do.

Jubbars hated the mailman for the daily invasion of his territory. A high wooden fence surrounded the mansion. The mailman had to put the newspapers and mail through a hole in the gate. I used to watch Jubbars from the kitchen window. He would get up and start walking back and forth just before the mailman was due. When I could see the mailman's hat over the fence, Jubbars would take up his position near the gate and then bark when he heard the mailman approaching.

One day, however, he waited for the mailman and tracked him along the fence until they got to the gate. When the mailman pushed the mail through the hole, Jubbars jumped up and snapped over the fence and got the mailman's hat. He tore it to shreds, while the mailman cursed and swore and yelled for the owners of "that stupid dog."

It was only after my Uncle Anton gave the mailman a bottle of vodka that Jubbars finally calmed down. But he refused to deliver the mail anymore through the slot, so my uncle told him to just throw it over the fence. From then on, that's what he did. Jubbars quit barking at him after that.

I didn't like my Uncle Anton very much because he was always talking about how good the government was and how well everything was going under Communism. "Sure," I thought, "he has everything he needs. He doesn't look around to see what's really going on."

One day he asked me, "Why are you wearing the same dress, Lilitchka? Put on another one." When I told him I had only one dress, he teased me about it. It was rude of him to bring up the subject of how many dresses I had. Although he was a decent man and a respected teacher, I visited as little as I could after that summer.

Soon after I went back to my family, I came home with a huge dog. I left him sitting on the steps outside; when mom appeared, he growled at her. She yelled out, "LILY?" I appeared and told her, "Mom, you come in. Don't worry. He is not biting people." Mom said, "Who is that?" I said, "It's a big dog; he came home with me. He will be living with us."

"No, Lily. He is NOT going to live with us. Where did you find him? Go to his street. He will go with you, and you must come home alone. If you come home with this dog again, I will leave you. I will leave you guys, all of you. I'll just disappear, and you will all be alone." It was frightening. I understood that Mom was really upset. I chose Mom instead of this dog. I said, "Okay, *suka blat*, let's go now." I grabbed him by the collar, took him to his neighborhood, pushed him into his yard, and closed the gate. He stared at me and started whining, wagging his tail as though he wanted to play. But I told him, "We do not have time to play with dogs, to dress them up as in America. We are survivors, we do not play games."

***

That fall Svetlana got very sick. I don't know what the problem was, but she was in bed a long time. I went into her room a lot, and always looked at her table to see whether Mom had left her any food. If she had, I asked, "How do you feel, Svetlana?"

She answered weakly, "Fine. Okay..."

Then I asked her, "Why don't you eat?"

"I don't want anything."

After this answer, I immediately ate the food Mom had left. Svetlana always smiled and said, "Okay, you can eat it, Lilia. Go ahead. I really don't want it." When I finished eating, I went right off to play or to do something else, figuring my duty towards her was finished.

One day, my father said, "Lilia, I am in a hurry. Please go to the store and buy me some of this sweet bread called *Kovritchka*. Can you remember that? Svetlana is not eating anything, and I am afraid that she needs something special. Please, do it for her." I was surprised he had asked me, because Mother would never have trusted me to go on such an errand.

I promised my father to get this bread and bring it to Svetlana. He gave me the money and the permission coupon and started getting ready for work. I didn't wait until he had left the house but I immediately got my coat and ran to the store. I waited in line for a long time for this bread and finally got it.

I chose a very long way back home, just to think and look around. I was walking along when I suddenly realized that this bread was in my hands. I looked in the bag at the bread, squeezed it and then reached in to touch it. I saw that it was a pretty big piece of bread and thought, "Svetlana doesn't need so much bread," so I broke off a little piece and ate it, then closed the bag.

A little further on, I looked at the bread again, and saw that it was very big, maybe even bigger than when I had bought it. "I can break off another piece and eat it." So I did. Then another piece, and another. Walking along, I tried to persuade myself that I'd eaten enough. "You can't do this, Lilia. Stop it. It's for Svetlana." But another voice was saying, "But she's sick. She's sick and doesn't want to eat anything. What's the problem with you?" I ate this bread down to the last crumb.

When I saw that the bread was completely gone, I got frightened. I was really scared, imagining the beating I would get. "Oh, no. This is it." I decided, "I really can't go home now. Nobody in the family will ever talk to me again." To save myself, I rushed to the home of my best friend, Lena Leiko.

Lena, her sister, and her mom lived in a teeny, dark, gloomy room with only one window looking out at a big wall. I found Lena and her sister alone, and the three of us played the whole evening. When her mother came home from sweeping floors in the local school, she was surprised to see me. "Lilia, why are you here? Look outside. It's nighttime. How will you get home?"

I looked outside. "Oh, yes, it's dark. I am afraid to go home in the dark. I guess I'll stay here tonight."

"No, Lilia, your mom will be looking for you, you know?" Nobody had a phone at this time in Russia. She said, "Get your coat, Lilia, very quickly, and I will accompany you to your home." Our apartment was not far away. On the way home, Lena's mom was watching me and finally said, "Lilia, what happened? Did you do something wrong? Why don't you want to go home?"

I said shamefully, "I ate my sick sister's bread, every bit of it. I don't know what to say or what to do. I don't want to go home."

She said, "It's okay, Lilia. You were hungry, that's all. It's okay." We arrived at our apartment. "Just open the door and admit you ate the bread. Ask to be forgiven. That's all, no more."

She pushed me up to the door, and I knocked. Mom opened it and said, "Hah! Here she is." She had a very serious expression on her face. I started to cry immediately and closed the door before Lena's mother could come in.

Mother said, "What's the problem? Where is the bread? Where have you been? Why didn't you come home? We were looking for you. We were worried about you." There was no patience, no compassion in her face or in her words. She was very, very angry.

I said, "I lost everything, I lost everything, the bread, the money, the permission slip, everything."

She looked at me and said, "Stop it. Stop it now and forever. Don't lie. I know you're hungry. I know you ate the bread. Please, I don't blame you for that. Just don't lie about it. Don't get in the habit of telling one lie after another. You are a hungry little girl, Lilia. I know that. I can't supply you with bread because there is not much bread in our country. But you must not lie."

I was very ashamed. I wished I'd admitted what I'd done, as Lena's mother had urged. I wished I'd admitted it right away because I saw that my family loved me and forgave me for what I had done. But I realized it too late. It was a very powerful lesson for me—either say nothing, but don't lie. I was young, but I understood this lesson for the rest of my life.

I also understood that my mom was very upset that she couldn't get enough bread for us. She wanted to hit me for taking Svetlana's bread, but she didn't. When she looked at me, she loved me instead. My sister was also very kind to me again. She asked mother, "Please don't beat her and don't lecture her. I knew she didn't come home because she ate the bread. It's not her fault. She's just stupid and hungry. Look at her. She is thin; she has shabby clothes. She doesn't even have her own nice dress. Please, stop it."

Svetlana was only four-and-a-half years older than me. She was a wonderful person. She took care of me during all the War years. She was just a little girl when we lived under the shed, and yet she washed me when I had diarrhea. Sure, she used cold water because there was nobody to warm the water up when I needed to be washed. I have always loved Svetlana. She was so smart, so serious, and always so upset about our family's struggles. She was like an angel.

In school, Svetlana was usually quiet, submissive, obedient, always getting 5's in all her classes; always and in every subject, she got the highest grade. She wrote a lot, and her compositions were unbelievable; even the faculty told her so. She wrote poems, beautiful poems, and songs, too. She was very talented and wrote poems even in her earlier school years. Her verses were wonderful. She was a good director for the school plays, too, with the nicest character, with no up-and-down moods, and she was very, very beautiful. But she paid no attention to boys nor to the attention she got from boys. It was not in our culture, especially after the War. We were hungry all the time, so we didn't think about boys. We thought about bread, a piece of bread.

One day I can remember Mom asking her, "Svetlana, how are you doing in chemistry?" Svetlana didn't like the chemistry teacher, who was always picking on her. Svetlana said to Mom, "You know, Mom, I *grezanola* her," which literally means "I bite her," and she told how she bit her: by abruptly responding to what the teacher was teaching. The chemistry teacher spoke about something, and Svetlana *grezanola* abruptly and the chemistry teacher was shocked and couldn't say anything. Svetlana had said something very funny. Svetlana showed that she was not so shy and silent as she appeared to be. She had a high level of self-confidence, but she did not express it too much. She knew what she was doing, knew what she was talking about, though she did not talk too much; she was always doing, and doing, and doing. The teacher did give her a 5 at the end of the semester. Mom said to her, "You *grezanola*'d her. Did the blood go to the ceiling?" Svetlana said, "Almost."

When she graduated from our school, she was admitted to the Moscow Architectural Institute, where she quickly became a most valuable contributor with her architectural project designs over the years. After she graduated, she went to work as an architect.

[Svetlana had a son who lived with her ex-husband in Leviv. Svetlana was not able to communicate with him for many years; her ex-husband prohibited it. Eventually this son also became an architect in urban design. At some point after Svetlana's death, this son came to Moscow and applied to the Moscow Architectural Institute, not knowing his mother had spent years there and had died before many of her wonderful projects could be implemented. When the son was interviewed, the manager told him that they had had a wonderful, talented woman who produced very creative projects that the manager would like someone to take over and implement. The son said he would like to do that and was immediately hired. After he started working on the projects, he discovered his mother's name on all the project blueprints! Eventually he became tired of Moscow and moved back to Leviv again.]

Only after Svetlana was about 28 did she get chronically sick. She had been so very frightened by what she saw in the War, but I was too young then to know what was going on. She was shocked by events, that the Germans found us, and that grandma had us running and hiding all the time. It traumatized Svetlana. She focused on caring for me all the time. This was not unusual in our country. Due to WWII people were severely frightened, were killed or imprisoned. I think she was an angel, but she suffered for it.

Later in life, I was absorbed with my activities, how to escape, how to run somewhere, how to find something to eat, where to steal something, maybe a doll, maybe a dog. I did not keep in close touch with Svetlana until after I graduated from college.

✳✳✳

Late that spring, when I was eleven, my mother took me back to her parents' village for the first time since the War ended. The shed was still there. Mother and I were out walking on a brilliant sunny morning when an old woman sitting on a bench seemed to recognize my mother and called out to us. She identified herself as "the policeman's mother." My mother said she did not know a policeman. The old woman was quiet. "My son was a policeman in this village during the War. One day he went to your mother's house and asked for your picture, implying that you were a Partisan. Your mother threatened and cursed him, so he left her house. But later on, he betrayed your daughters."

This old woman said that her long-held hope was to see my mother before her death so she could ask for forgiveness for her son, who had been killed as a collaborator after the war ended. "Please, if you will only forgive me, I can die easily." My mother forgave her, and this old woman couldn't stop thanking my mother and kissing her hand.

After a few days, my mother went home. I stayed with Grandma Anna for the rest of the summer. One of Grandma's hens hatched eleven chicks, but the hen cared for only ten of them and tried to drive the last one out. I showed my fist to this hen, and took the little chick inside and gave it something to eat. I watched over the chick for several days. Then Grandma Anna spoke to me about this little chick.

"That chick is following you around, Lilia. It thinks you are its mother. There is no one to teach it to eat worms, so you must feed it and take care of it until it grows up, or it will die. I will boil an egg, and you cut it up and feed it to the chick."

That chick followed me everywhere. Sometimes I would be playing, forget about the chick, and run far ahead of it. But it would make a noise, and I would slow down until it caught up with me. Occasionally I would go up to the chick's mother hen with a stick, and ask, "Why do you peck at your own child?" I poked the hen with my stick. "Why are you so mean to this little chick who never did anything to you?" I poked her again. "Why do you drive her away?" One more poke. "Now I am her mother, and I will protect her, do you hear?"

One morning, I decided to teach the chick to eat worms. I took it outside, got a stick and dug around with it, and found a big, long worm. The worm scared the chick, so it ran away and all the other chicks came over and fought over this worm. But gradually this little chick got the idea to eat the worms I dug for her.

At first she could only hop, and not too high. She could not get up the five steps into the house. I would hold out my palm for her, and the chick would come over and look, then move back a few steps, and come bouncing up and jump into my hand. So I lifted her up onto the first step. Then I would hold out my palm again, and the chick jumped in so I could lift her to the second step. It took a long time to get up those steps, but eventually she could do it herself. This was the only chicken Grandma let into the house.

She grew up quickly, becoming a wonderful hen who laid one egg each day, which I collected for Grandma. "She looks different, doesn't she?" asked Grandma. "Look how her tail is short, and she is fatter than the rest. I think that she was someone else's chick and that her egg got mixed in with the others." I didn't care. It still seemed unfair.

Lilia's father, Vladimir, a major in the Resistance,
from <u>Government Archives</u>

Lilia's 11-year-old brother Anatoly (Tolya) in the Resistance,
Government Archives

Lilia's mother, Marie, asleep on a cart, a nurse in the Resistance,
<u>Government Archives</u>

Lilia's brother, Anatoly, who became a military journalist, signing his book on the Resistance. He is responsible for finding the above Resistance pictures in the <u>Government Archives</u>.

Lilia's mother, Marie, back in Moscow, family photo

Lilia's father, Vladimir, history teacher, family photo

Lilia's sister, Svetlana, 23-years-old, family photo

Lilia at 19-years-old, Moscow University, family photo

7

The Atheism Course (1952)

My first course in the eighth grade was Atheism. The textbook started with a chapter that said there was no God, and that the God my Grandmother Anna had told me about did not exist. The teacher commented, "The idea of a god was created a thousand years ago by the bourgeois to suppress people's freedom and keep them in slavery. But right now in Russia, we are a truly free people, because we have gotten rid of those who believe in a god. That's why here in this class, no one believes in God."

The teacher pointed to a boy in the first seat. "Isn't that right, Sergei? Sergei, stand up." Sergei stood up, and the teacher asked him, "Do you believe in God, Sergei?"

Sergei shouted, "No! I don't!" The teacher began asking each of us, one by one, to stand and answer this question. Of course we all stood up and betrayed God with certainty and enthusiasm, for fear that all our family would be sent off to a prison camp in Siberia.

That was our introduction. Then we studied the absence of God in the universe. "The universe is just a physical and astronomical essence. Where is there a place for a god to live? Nowhere! There's only an empty universe out there." It seemed very scientific.

The second chapter was about Lenin. "Lenin is our ideal. We truly believe in his teachings." On and on about Lenin, how he was a saint, how he struggled with the czar, with the White Army, with the whole regime in Russia, and how all his opponents were finally destroyed in the great October Revolution. Then more about Lenin, and more, till I was sick of hearing about him. We also studied the lives of the Bolsheviks and their leaders. They were presented as heroes, examples of the wonderful theory of Leninism. My father told me that a lot of the Bolsheviks had already been killed in Stalin's purges.

There were fifty or sixty pages on these themes, then, abruptly "Stalin was Lenin's pupil. Stalin studied all of Lenin and he is also our hero. All he does is for the good of Russia." For the rest of the book, we had to study Stalinism and Stalin, all his works, and all his speeches. My father told me Stalin never wrote any of them, that he was illiterate and was kicked out of a Georgian seminary because of his "inappropriate behavior," that he was really a murderer and a maniac.

The Atheism book stated that there was no evidence of any type of god. But mostly it was a book praising Lenin and Stalin, whom we had to trust without any doubts or evidence. We were taught that we had to believe in the two saints, Stalin and Lenin, or go to Hell in prison.

Stalin's picture was always in the newspapers, and I got in the habit, while I was taking the Atheism class, of poking holes in his newspaper eyes with my finger. One day my father saw it and said, "Oh no, Lilia. If these are found in our trash, we would be in great trouble. They can trace the newspaper back to our house. To have holes in Stalin's eyes, to draw on his face...it is better to burn this paper. But don't throw it in the trash." That's where I got the idea to burn my Atheism book in our back yard.

We finally finished this Atheism book and received a grade. I didn't think I would get a "Fail" and felt I would surely get a "Pass" or maybe a "Good." But I got an "Excellent," because I had a wonderful memory; I could repeat whole pages by heart without any mistakes, repeating everything with a dumb, dull face. For this I got an "Excellent."

Once the course was over, we were told we had to have Lenin's volumes in our homes, all thirty-three of them. If your home was checked and the volumes were not there, you would be under great suspicion.

So I came home that last day, holding my Atheism book. I looked around my father's books, and saw we had a lot of Lenin's works at our house, maybe forty-five volumes. I decided, "We have enough books on Lenin. We don't need any more." So I took my book out in our back yard, which had a tall fence and bushes around it and was very secluded. I found some branches and put them in a little pile and very methodically tore out the pages of Atheism and put them on the branches.

I went into the kitchen and got some matches, but my sister Svetlana saw me. "What are you doing, Lilia? I know you are doing something. You are always getting in trouble." She shook her finger at me. "Tell me what you're doing."

I already had the matches, so I put on my classroom face and said "Nothing," and casually walked outside. She did not follow me, so I made a wonderful fire.

I was so very angry at this class. It was so boring, and every lesson was the same. The teacher had terrified and intimidated us. I couldn't express these feelings to my closest friends. I had to go to class, sit and nod my head, and look straight into the teacher's eyes and express with my own eyes that I so truly believed in Lenin, so truly and so intensely. I even dropped my mouth open with such awe for Lenin. But all the while I was thinking, "Jeeze, you stupid idiot, when will this be over? When will it be over? Oh my God, will this stupid Lenin ever end? Will this lesson ever be finished?"

That semester Stalin and Lenin were injected into every subject: botany, astronomy, even Russian literature. When we studied Pushkin, we had to talk about Stalin and Lenin, how Stalin had influenced Pushkin, how Lenin had influenced Pushkin, even though Pushkin had lived centuries earlier. Such stupidity you cannot imagine. All the physics classes, all the chemistry classes, even the reading classes--all of them were filled with Stalin and Lenin. It made us lead two lives in order to survive, one life inside ourselves, and one life outside where Stalinism and Leninism were.

The real Stalinists and Leninists were members of the ruling Communist Party. My first real contact with them occurred when I was about fourteen.

All my school friends were as poor as me, and in this way we were all equal. The school required the girls in all the grades to wear a brown dress and a black apron, which you washed and ironed and always wore; for special celebrations and ceremonies, we added a white apron, a white collar and white cuffs. Whoever could get this uniform from a store, bought it. Whoever was not able to buy a uniform got materials and sewed their own. It was very nice because we were all the same at school. Of course some girls had wonderful uniforms sewn from rich material, and other girls had nothing, just a plain homemade brown dress and black apron.

There was a group of students who were rich, those in the highest ranks of the Communist Party. They were always together, and they were always arrogant. They seemed to hate all of us who were poor and shabbily dressed, who had holes in our long, drooping stockings, which we tied onto our thighs with cotton string. Whenever one of us passed these students, one of them would laugh loudly and talk about us. They teased me by talking about my Mom's job, about how she worked at a restaurant selling cutlets and counting money. This was how they tortured me. They enjoyed laughing and teasing us all, trying to humiliate us in any possible way, especially in class where the teachers tolerated their behavior because the teachers too were afraid of being sent to prison.

It was the procedure in many Russian schools for a student to go to the front of the class and stand next to the teacher any time you spoke, for example, to read a poem about Lenin or Stalin or the Communist Party. Many students felt ashamed and upset after reciting, but not me. I understood that my failure at any time in front of any class would be a reason for these arrogant students to put me down. I made up my mind that nobody would get the chance to laugh at me just because I didn't know something. There were enough normal reasons to laugh at me--because I was tall, shabbily dressed, ugly, without shoes, and without proper clothes. So I eliminated anything else by doing a wonderful job in my classes. And I was doing very well. Chemistry class in high school was no problem for me. I had a very good memory, and if you could remember everything, it was no problem to get a five in general chemistry and even in organic chemistry. It was absolutely no problem, in high school and in college.

Chemistry, geometry, algebra: no problem. Only physics was a problem for me.

The Russian educational system was very demanding, requiring that we learn many subjects and Communist Party history. We had to learn Lenin, Lenin, Lenin, Stalin, Stalin, Bolsheviks and their enemies--the Aristocracy. We were taught that whoever was against the Bolsheviks should be dead. These classes were often frightening.

Very rarely, the teacher presented the work of a real Russian poet. When a Lermentov poem was suddenly introduced to us one day, I went home and learned this wonderful poem by heart from the beginning to the end. The next day during class discussion, the teacher asked for our opinion of this poem. I raised my hand, came up next to the teacher's desk, and described this poem about a man who had escaped from a monastery, and had run through the forest to his freedom. I thought it was a wonderful poem. When the teacher asked what impressed me the most, I answered, "Freedom."

She was shocked at the intensity of my answer. She looked at me and asked, "What do you mean, Freedom?"

I answered, "Freedom is the essence of this poem." Then I began to recite the poem from the beginning. The whole class was stunned that someone could remember all of this poem. The teacher stared at me but did not stop me, so I kept on reciting. The bell rang at the end of class, but nobody moved until I finished the poem. The group of arrogant students neither laughed at me during my recitation, nor tried to humiliate me afterwards in their usual style. The teacher said "Bravo. Wonderful, Lilia. You did a wonderful job." And she spoke a few sentences about real poetry. She told us just a little more about Lermentov, a true Russian poet.

I secretly hoped to get a Golden Medal at graduation for my school work. I did not yet know that the Golden Medal was intended only for the Communist Party children. But the main reason I studied was not for the medal, but so I wouldn't be humiliated for not knowing something.

A few days after my reciting the Lermentov poem, I was walking around between classes when I passed two girls who began laughing loudly at me. They were standing on a staircase with nobody around. It was too much for me. I quickly turned and punched both of them. I said, "I will kill you if you continue to laugh at me. I will just kill you. So remember." I punched them several more times, convinced it would be enough to stop their teasing.

But after my next class, I was sent home with a note asking my mother to please bring me to school immediately to see the director. When we got back to school, the director gave her an address and said, "You and your daughter must go to this address to apologize and to settle this very serious matter. A very serious matter, indeed!"

Mom took my hand and we started walking to this address. We walked silently for about five minutes; then Mom turned to me. "Okay, Lilitchka, tell me frankly. What...did...you...do? Speak completely truthfully, without any lie, because it's very serious. I think this is the address of the secretary of the local Communist Party. I'm afraid it is."

I said, "Nothing, mother. I...I just beat two girls who were laughing at me because I am poor. And I am tired of being poor, tired of not having proper shoes. I am tired of not having a coat, not having dresses, Mom. I am just tired of it. That's all. I never told you about this. I know that we are poor because of the War, because we lost everything. I know that. I do not demand anything, I am not asking for anything. But I am tired of being laughed at."

She said, "Okay. It's clear to me. That's enough. Stop it." We went home first, and Mom told the rest of the family what happened, and gave them instructions on what to do if she and Lilia didn't return in three hours. She was quite fearful that we might be sent to prison.

When we arrived at the address about a half hour later, we were stunned. In front of us was a huge building, set apart with white columns and an iron fence around it. There was a militiaman with a rifle standing in front. He asked us who we were, wrote our names on a list, and called inside. Finally he passed us through the gate, and into an elegant home.

The floors were parquet; windows and glass were everywhere. One of the girls I had punched came down from the second floor in a wonderful nightgown covered with a silk robe. Her mother came in from another room, an attractive woman, good looking and young, and wearing a wonderful dress. She addressed my mother as we stood facing each other.

"Come in, please," she said to mother. "I'd like to speak to you. My daughter is so upset by what happened that she has refused to go to school. She is afraid of your daughter. Your daughter beat her. I don't know the reason. My daughter said she did nothing, that your daughter was passing by her and her friend, and just turned and began to punch them and beat them severely. So my daughter has refused to go to school."

"You know, I haven't told my husband. If I were to do so, I am afraid there would be grave consequences for you and for your family." She spoke slowly and quietly.

My mom got pale. She was quiet for a few more moments before she spoke. "Okay. I'd like to explain the reason why my daughter beat your daughter—because your daughter laughed at her for being poor, for not having proper clothes, for not having shoes. I deeply apologize for that. I deeply apologize that we are poor." My mother had a very sharp tongue and a very keen mind. With a humble face and a look of deep regret, she slowly said "I think that 90% of our country is poor right now. It's nobody's fault; it was a result of the War. The War killed many of us, destroyed our cities, destroyed the factories. Right now we are in the process of rebuilding. We hope for a bright future, but not right now. Right now we are poor. I deeply, deeply apologize for that, I don't know how to express my deep sorrow for being poor." My mother looked this woman straight in the eyes.

I got cold. I understood that this situation was not simple, but more like a struggle between the two classes in our Russia. This woman suddenly spoke, "I'm sorry. Okay, I understand. It's not a big deal. I'll talk with my daughter. She will never, never laugh at your daughter again. I must apologize for my daughter. You know, I feel that this matter is settled, and I'd like the girls not to be enemies. I hope that your daughter never beats my daughter again. It's not a proper action."

My mom responded, "Yes, it's true. It's not a proper action. Absolutely. I agree with that, I agree completely, and I will talk with Leonila promptly and ask her not to do it again." She reached for my hand, but continued to face the lady. "I will ask her not to fight with anyone, not with your daughter or with anyone else." We turned to leave.

The woman invited us to stay and have tea, but my mom strictly refused, "Oh no, we are in a hurry, a big hurry." So we opened the door and went out through the gate past the militia man with the rifle.

I walked with my mom, looking sideways at her in silence. When we had left that neighborhood, my mom began to laugh a bit, but very squeakily, very restrained, almost to herself. "You know, Lilia," she said quietly, "we beat them. We beat them physically and emotionally, and you know what? We won. We won." We were smiling.

When we got home, we laughed openly. Svetlana and Anatoly and my dad joined in. My mother acted out the conversation, what each one had said and how the other had responded. We laughed and were so happy. We beat not only the daughter of the communist party leader, but his wife. I beat them physically and mom beat them psychologically. It was dangerous.

***

Then Stalin died! It was 1953 and I was fourteen. I was at school when I heard the news. At the beginning of the first class, our teacher, Maria Ivanovna, came into the room and we all stood up as usual. She paused and looked around at us, then announced in a deep sorrowful voice, with tears in her eyes, "Our father has died."

She could not say anything more, because our class erupted into a big panic; we cried and yelled and asked, "Who died? My father was alive this morning. What's happened? What's happened? My father was fine when I left for school. My father died in the War; how could he die again?" We were all yelling and asking.

Maria Ivanovna responded sternly, in a very high-pitched voice. "You are stupid, all of you. Who cares if all of your fathers die. It's the great Father of us all who has died, the same Father for all of us."

I yelled out "Not my father. He is different from your father. He didn't die." And another girl said, "My father is different too. Who died?"

The teacher said, "The great Father of all the Russian people, Stalin, died. Now all of you have to go over to the portrait of Stalin in pairs," and she pointed at the first two students. "Stay there without any movement, even without blinking your eyes, for 20 minutes. Then the next pair will go. We'll change every twenty minutes until everyone has stood there in turn. The rest of you must cry. If you are not crying, I will report you to the Director, who will report you to you-know-who, and she raised her hands toward the ceiling. We all knew whom she had in mind—the KGB. So we started our rotation next to the portrait.

I was terrified because I was sure I would probably start laughing after this pressure to conform. I bent over as though I were in pain and moaned, and told the teacher my stomach was hurting me and I needed to go immediately to the bathroom because I had diarrhea. She sneered at me, "During this tragic event, who cares if you have diarrhea. Get out of here right now."

She waved me out of the classroom. I went to the bathroom and hid in a stall, raising my feet up so no one would see me and send me back to the class. I waited for a long while, until I thought my turn to stand had passed. Then I went back into class.

All the students were sitting at their desks, crying and whimpering. I could not squeeze one tear from my eyes. This was dangerous, because the teachers were watching our reactions. So I covered my eyes with my hand and made crying sounds. I put my head down on the desk, put a finger into my mouth and put spit under my eyes for tears. I rubbed my eyes until they were red.

We sat solemnly and sadly most of the school day, while the teachers talked about the great tragedy of Stalin's death and played classical music that was solemn and sad. It was the first time I had heard such wonderful music. "The great Stalin is dead. He was our most loved hero." But I knew that my father had told me the truth.

When I came home, my mom was crying in the kitchen, and the next moment my father came in mumbling to himself, but we could hear him, "Thank God he's dead. His carcass rots at last. He is dead, and his carcass is finally rotting." He kept repeating it, "He's dead. His carcass rots at last." I saw him fall slowly to his knees and cross himself, and put his forehead on the floor, repeating these phrases.

Suddenly he raised his head and looked at us sitting there. "Maria, why are you crying? Why are you crying at his dead carcass? Don't be stupid."

"Everyone is crying, Vladi," she moaned. My mother was being a good Russian citizen. "Everyone else is crying, too."

"That's because the only people left in this country are the stupid ones, Maria. Stalin killed 60 million Russians and claimed it was for the motherland that he rid the country of everybody who could think. Thank God he's dead now, Maria, thank God."

Anatoly and Svetlana came from school just then, and Anatoly was very elated and shouted, "I'm so happy—Stalin died, so tomorrow we won't have classes. I can sleep until twelve and no school." Mom tried to silence him for fear someone would hear him.

We had our usual standard potato soup for supper that evening. I ended up alone at the table with Mom, so she gave me another helping of soup, and I thought, "Maybe tomorrow some other important government official will die, and I'll get another extra bowl of soup."

People thought power would eventually pass to Berea, one of Stalin's henchmen, a short man like Stalin, only more cruel. Everyone feared him.

But shortly after Stalin's death, a man named Kruschev, who had fought in Ukraine, executed a coup and put Berea in prison, where he was quickly killed. Once Kruschev was in power, an order came down to my father to make an inspection of the prison school system and then to improve it.

After developing the school system, father returned and told us that he had found many inmates willing to teach, and all of them had PhD's. He said he had met great numbers of wonderful, educated people in the prisons: engineers and historians. He took them out of the workforce in the forests and in the mines and made them teachers of mathematics and Russian literature for the rest of the prisoners, most of whom did not seem like criminals. My father was in a state of despair about Russia, having witnessed for himself that anyone with education and a trace of culture had been imprisoned.

I asked him if there was something we could do to help our country. He was frustrated and said, "No. Just get a Kalishnikoff and *go to the barricades.*" This expression came from the 1917 October Revolution when the peasants *"went to the barricades"* to fight against the czarist regime. Most people had forgotten this expression, but not my father. "*Go to the barricades,*" he repeated. "I would die there, shooting at the communists. It's the only way to save Russia now."

My Dad's prison school system worked very well and he was proud of it. Five years later, after Kruschev's prisoner amnesty program went into effect, many educated people released from prison came to our house, and we often went to theirs. They always expressed their gratitude for my father's actions and told many stories long into the night.

I remember one technologist who would not drink vodka. He told me that he had helped design and manufacture several new types of tanks during WWII. He said he was in charge of a factory at Chelyabinsk in the Urals. There were no young adults around to work in the factory because they were all fighting in the War. So he ended up hiring a lot of eleven-, twelve- and thirteen-year-olds. When he found out that most of them were orphaned during the War or had parents in prison, he fed them from factory funds and let them sleep on the factory floor. He gave them extra pay for working two shifts in a row.

He proudly revealed that his factory was often praised for being the most productive during the War. He spoke fondly about several of the youth who had worked for him. But when the War ended, he was accused of stealing from the state because he had helped these kids, and that's how he ended up in the prison where my dad found him.

8

Boys

In general, I hated boys. I was tall and skinny and ugly, and they teased me a lot. I fought with them every chance I got. I was happy to have my brother in the same school because he was seven years older than me. It was enough to have a big brother in school so that nobody would ever, ever touch me. And everybody knew him because he played football for the school, ran track, and participated in a lot of other sports.

The school required uniforms for both boys and girls. The boys wore a white shirt and sometimes a tie, white or grey pants and a jacket, so they looked very professional. They were never shabbily dressed and behaved themselves in school. There was no fighting or playing around in school. Outside of school, however, they were yelling, screaming, beating each other, as usual for boys. But when they came inside for school, none of that was tolerated. There was very strict discipline in the Russian school system, and I liked this discipline. They told us we were there to learn, to behave, and to prepare ourselves. School was like a style of life. None of the older boys ever disobeyed the discipline and, as far as I remember, never needed punishing for disobeying. It was very unusual for anyone to openly disobey authority in Russia.

All the classes in the school were small, because there were not so many kids after the War. Our classes never had more than 20 students, never. Usually there was a smaller number, and we got lots of attention from our teachers because there were not many of us left after the War. We young people were usually frightened of the older kids, frightened to even look at them. I think the older kids said to themselves that "finally I am in class in a school, and I want to learn something." That was a very nice generation; they went through ordeals during the War, including my brother, Tolya.

At home my brother was funny, joking all the time. We had moved to a suburban area; however, there was still no food there either, and it was difficult. But Tolya went around the town and came home with food for us. We didn't know where he got this food, but he brought apples, other fruit, and some vegetables. He found carrots and potatoes; he always tried to bring something for us. He never ever said even a single word about the War and what he had done, his role in it, just like my mom and my dad who never talked about the War either. The kids age 9-12 at the start of the War, were a wonderful generation, and were very much admired for their bravery and helpfulness.

When I was a little fourth grader, I liked a boy named Sergei from my brother's tenth-grade class. I never talked to Sergei, but I watched and admired him because he was pretty handsome. He always wore a white shirt and tie and a gray suit to school. He came to our house often with my brother and never paid any attention to me. But I liked him. He was my ideal man with his nice clothes and neat haircut. I don't know if he was smart or not.

After fourth grade, I had a lot of friends who were boys, but we never thought of dating. We just ran around together, played dodge ball, and fought.

Even in high school, I usually ignored boys. I was very studious. I had decided to go to Moscow University, and I needed very good grades. My father supported and encouraged me, but it was I who decided to study so hard. I wanted to be educated. I wanted to know; I wanted to be someone.

There was a popular boy named Victor in my second-year class. He was the star in our school, and every girl dreamed of dating him. At this time in Russia, a date meant walking together along the street for about an hour, then seeing a movie and walking home. Victor was tall and played soccer pretty well. He was very famous in school and definitely handsome.

No one thought I was beautiful at this time. If a girl was tall, she was ugly by definition. The Russian standard of beauty was to be small and plump, but I was tall and slim with very long bright brown hair, which I wore below my shoulders. My Mom told me I was pretty, but I didn't think I was at all, because my peers didn't think so. I was never called names to my face because people knew I would beat them up if they did. Maybe they talked behind my back, but I never heard it.

There were only twenty of us in the sophomore class after the War, twelve boys and eight girls. One day when I came into the classroom, I noticed the other students were exchanging little notes with each other, whispering things and laughing. I noticed that some of the girls looked at me after reading these notes. But when I looked at them, they stopped looking at me. If I pretended not to look at them, they began to giggle. And I decided, "Uh-oh. Something's going on. I have to be alert."

Sometime before the last lesson, this guy Victor sent me a note. It said, "Would you mind seeing me this evening at Central Park on the north side of the skating pond at eight o'clock?"

My first reaction was "Oh sure, sure." I was thrilled because, wow, the star of the school asked me for a date. I wrote a note saying okay and sent it back to him. I saw that he showed this note to the student next to him, and they read it together, which triggered my second doubt about what was going to happen.

Once I got home, I suddenly asked myself, "Why did this guy suddenly decide to make a date with me? What the heck is going on?" I recalled that recently he was dating Svetlana Bandachuk. She was pretty as a doll, and her parents were very rich. She had beautiful dresses and shoes and was shorter, with black eyes and black hair, more the standard beauty. I had no pretty clothes, only a uniform. My parents were teachers with a miserable salary, so my sister and brother and I didn't dress very well at all.

I decided, "No, no, something is wrong here. Okay, I will go, but I will go much earlier than eight o'clock." I left for the park at six o'clock, two hours early.

There were huge bushes around the place where we were to meet, and I hid myself in the deepest bushes, waiting and thinking about Victor's actions over and over again. Then, about seven-thirty, I suddenly saw people coming into view, people from my class. I saw my classmates walk through this meeting place and hide behind the nearby trees.

"Oh my god," I thought, "I see what's going on. He'd just like to laugh at me." I didn't know exactly what he was intending, but I figured he had some scheme to humiliate me. I waited ten or fifteen minutes more because I had a really good hiding place. More classmates arrived, so I crawled backwards on the ground and down a little hill. At the bottom, I stood up and then ran home.

I don't know what else happened that night, but the next day when I came to school, Victor was waiting for me with some of his friends. "Lilia," he called to me. I stopped and looked at him. "Why didn't you come yesterday? I was waiting for you for more than an hour." He looked casually at me and waited for my reply.

"You know why I didn't come?" I answered. "Because you are just a stupid idiot, that's why. I don't care if you waited for me or anybody else. I don't care. You think you're a star, but in reality you are nothing, you know? You are stupid; you never answer a single question in class correctly. How could I come to you? Can't you understand that you are just a pig, always dirty, always stupid. Look at yourself." That was all I said. I walked away.

It was like an explosion all over the school. Everybody talked about that incident, and I suddenly turned into a real celebrity. Before my outburst, all the girls just died whenever Victor looked at them. They would faint if he beckoned them and were immediately ready to go on a date. But, after that, everything changed.

Several years later at our second high-school reunion, I came as the lone representative from Moscow University. Victor couldn't come, but his friends were there. All of us talked and laughed together, remembered, and enjoyed ourselves.

Toward the end of the evening, I was talking alone with one of Victor's friends, Boris Boynko. He told me, "You know, Lilia, I remember that day when you told Victor that he was a stupid idiot and a pig. You got a lot of respect by doing that. After that, nobody even thought about laughing at you anymore. It made me realize how beautiful and different you were compared to all the other girls. I can't say I loved you, but I really admired you. And now look at you. You are at the University. You have become so beautiful and modern and everything. I knew it."

I saw Boris again two year later and he said that he had spoken to Victor about me, and that Victor had said, "If you see Lilia again some day, please apologize for me."

This event in high school marked my first fight for myself, for my image, and for my independence. I was not like the typical Russian, but I said to myself, "No problem, this is me."

***

When Anatoly graduated from high school, he went to a military medical school, because when he was in the Partisan troop, he once met a famous general among the Partisans. This general asked Anatoly what he was going to do after the War. My brother said that he wanted to go to military medical school because his mother was a military nurse. He wanted to be a nurse or a doctor. The general replied to him, "OK. When this War is over, and you are in school and then graduate, come to me, and I will get you into a military medical school." So that was what my brother did after he graduated.

After he finished this military medical academy, he was posted to East Germany as a doctor. The Americans were in West Germany, and the Russians were in East Germany, so he was not in the middle of a war zone and was doing okay. Tolya had a few friends who occasionally went to Moscow. He had these friends bring me a few items, like a dress, some perfume, or some other presents. In this way, he continued to "bring things home" even after he graduated. And it was interesting that my mother's brother was also in East Germany, not far from Anatoly, so the two of them saw each other frequently.

When my brother and sister left for college or university, I was alone at home. But I still had my friends, and we just kept playing together. My brother was not like a friend; he was just family. So I was not so sad when he left because I was closer to my friends, and we were still together. My brother was older than me by seven years, so it is hard to explain. We were not friends; we were relatives. It was not a big tragedy when one of the family left home; the rest of the family just kept going.

9

University Dreams (1956)

To make some extra money during the summer months, Mother took students into the house, and put us kids in the attic to sleep, which was different and exciting. These students had just graduated from high school. They came from collective farms in small villages far from Moscow. They wanted to get into vocational-trade schools to learn to be electricians, plumbers, business workers, and lots of other lines of work.

Right after their graduation from high school, all students got a five-week internal passport to travel within the Soviet Union to try to get into a college or vocational-technical school by passing standardized exams. Each particular school picked three or four subjects to focus on, depending on what trade they were training students to enter. The colleges offered a month-long preparation course prior to these exams. Many local families opened their homes to these students, and all these host families were sympathetic to the pressure these students were under to do well.

Most of the students who stayed at our house said they didn't want to work all their lives on the collective farms, and were terrified that they would fail. Most of them studied hard, but they didn't know the basics and didn't really know how to learn things. But they brought good food with them, so I told them I'd pass the exam for them if they would give me some of their food. I was tall, looked older, and acted smart, so several students jumped at my offer. I started taking their exams and signing their names. I always passed because I had had a good education.

Several of the girls who got into local colleges told me a few weeks after starting school that their teachers were asking, "What happened to that tall, smart girl with the long blond hair? She couldn't have failed. Where is she?"

I even took a German exam for my father during the last summer. His diploma had been lost during the War, but he wrote to all his colleges and was able to get all of his transcripts except for his German course. He was told he would have to take an exam to prove his competence. But he was too busy, so I took the preparatory course for a month, and memorized the lessons well enough to pass, even though I couldn't speak German at all. I signed the test "V. Roussak." When my Dad got the letter saying he had passed, he just laughed and shook his head. He received another letter acknowledging his full diploma as a University history teacher.

I finished high school in 1957 and, as I had always dreamed, applied to the great Moscow University in the Biology Department. I was so elated, glad, and full of dreams about what it would be like, who the students would be. But the most exciting thing was that Moscow University had two campuses. The old one was situated in the historic center of Moscow, built about three hundred years ago. The buildings were old, with colonnades that impressed me. But the new building was on Leninsky Mountain overlooking the Moscow River at its base. This building was finished in 1953, so it was only three or four years old. The newspaper was full of articles about this new campus, about how happy the students were, how wonderfully they lived. Every student, it was written, had a small but separate room. The new buildings housed the faculty for chemistry, biology, math and geography. Each discipline had a separate building.

To get into university, you were required take four or five exams: Math, Physics, Chemistry, Russian composition, and a language, either English, French, or German. I took the English exam because in the suburbs, they taught mostly German. When we moved to Moscow, Moscow offered only English.

You had to pass each exam with a grade of 4 or 5. The exams were about poets and World War II, what was being done in the Communist Party, who were the heroes. I had no trouble writing about the Communist Party because I did not tell the truth. I just repeated whatever I had heard on the radio or read in the newspapers. If you did that and wrote a couple of sentences about the Communist Party, you easily got a 5 on your essay. So, without any strain, I wrote how the Communist Party took care of me, how we are the happiest people in the whole world now. Even if you had grammar mistakes and misspellings, it was not a problem to get a 5. I passed my exams for the University easily with 5's. If you included those few sentences about the Communist Party and got only a 3, you could complain, and they would change your score to a 5. Even in the Math exam, you had to put something about the Communist Party, or no 5. That's it.

In my Physics exam, I got only a 3, which was good enough, but I hated Physics. When I was learning it, I really didn't want to understand it. Even now, I still think there are only three laws in physics: (1) the law of conservation of energy; (2) energy can transform from one form to another; (3) mass converts to energy. The rest of the laws are disastrous. I was very good at geometry and algebra, so those subjects would have been no problem, but the fourth exam for me was not math but chemistry. And I loved chemistry, so that exam was nothing. It was an easy 5.

I learned poetry from reading my father's books that he saved from being burned and which we had hidden in the house; I could remember poetry easily. If the teacher asked us who knew Lermontov or Pushkin, everybody had heard about them; we knew that Pushkin was the best poet in Russian literature. Lermontov was a rebellious poet. When Pushkin was killed, Lermontov wrote a poem about Pushkin being killed by people who were around the czar.

One day, our teacher ordered us to learn a long Lermontov poem, or at least the first part or the last part. Next day, when the teacher asked if anyone read Lermontov, I put up my hand and said that I had learned it, and the teacher said, "Lily, what part of the poem did you learn?" I told her, "From the beginning to the end." She said, "OK, could you start at the beginning?" So I started it off. Then she said, "Ok, now go to the middle." Which I did. Then she told me to go to the end, which I did. So the teacher said she would put me down for a 5 for the whole quarter, and I didn't need to learn anything more— she would still give me a 5!

Actually, I already had memorized Lemontov, Maria Svetaeva, Anna Ahkmatova, and Blok. You know, my head was already filled with really rich poetry rather than stuff from the Communist Party. My father got me the books, and I learned them all. The four tests required at Moscow University were in biology, English (so I could read scientific literature), Russian composition, and chemistry. The minimum score for acceptance was 18 (out of 20), and I passed. I was accepted. I knew I would not go to a trade school, but that, instead, would have the best chance for a real career in biology.

The day before I was to start classes, I decided I was now grown up and not a child any more. I took my only doll and buried her in the back yard. But that night I dug her back up and apologized to her and went to bed, but I didn't sleep very well.

To start University, Mom sent me a bright green dress and some money for shoes. I went out, shopped everywhere, and found some bright red shoes. They were very big and long because my feet were long. I wore this dress all year long. My hair was very long, and I braided it behind me. My ears stuck out, and some curls fell over my forehead. I was still almost a foot taller than most of the kids who showed up for class.

I started my University career on September 1, 1957. I didn't know anyone in the Biological College. All the new students arrived on time and found a huge opening-day reception, with speeches and food. Everyone was greeted and shown much respect. We were so excited, just trembling and looking around, waiting for the doors to open so we could start our classes. At the end of the outdoor greeting, we were allowed to go into a big lecture hall, with its wonderful huge windows. There was so much light and air; everything was parquet, amazing and unforgettable. It gave me a sense of being part of something beautiful, something historical, something very old but very new and beautiful. In this wonderful mood, we started our classes at Moscow University.

Within two or three days, the loudspeakers announced that, because of rain and a lack of workers, all first-year students were to go to the Caucasus to work on a collective farm to gather the Russian harvest from the fields. Our

Russian harvest is the potato, and September is the time to get the potatoes from the fields lest the rain and snow soon come and destroy them, and everyone would be without any potatoes, our main crop. It was very important that they be harvested.

We were told to go home and get everything we would need, like boots, heavy pants, and a warm coat, and to come back to the University at nine o'clock the next morning, when buses would take us to the collective farm. It was announced that our work would be for only two weeks. So I went home to prepare.

I gathered what I had: my school uniform and shoes, a pair of blue sandals, my red sweatshirt, a scarf and a couple pair of socks. The next day I went back to school. A few of my classmates arrived with rubber boots to protect them from the rain. It was still warm and sunny in Moscow at that time, so I wasn't thinking about cold and rain. Besides, I didn't have any rubber boots or a warm winter coat, or work pants, or work shoes—nothing like that.

Sunday morning we were ready, waiting on the square for the buses. It was a wonderful warm and sunny day, and nothing seemed to be bad, so we were laughing and joking, ready for the trip. We finally had the chance to get acquainted with each other so we were laughing and urging each other on, "Good! Come on! Let's go gather these potatoes!" We did not realize how many potatoes we would have to gather in a very short period of time.

We all boarded long buses and were driven off the campus with music from a band and much encouragement from officials. We were singing the whole way. There were upper-class students on each bus who knew a lot of special university songs with great melodies, and they taught us how to sing those songs. They had a guitar and an accordion, and we were all singing. We were so young and full of hope for our future.

We headed to the collective farm in the Caucasus and arrived that evening in heavy rain and wind. The busses dropped us off at the bus station near the potato fields, and we had to walk the rest of the way. At first, they placed us with local families, two or three girls or boys with each family. But later they moved us into a big barn on the collective, usually used for the summer animals. The girls were on one side and the boys on the other, with just a sheet hung for privacy when we changed our baggy old underwear.

Picking potatoes in the cold rain was nasty, dirty work. We stood all day in a mud pond, and we were soon coughing all the time and very seriously. Nobody could stop, and a coughing spell could last a long time. It was hard work, and we were cold and hungry. They gave us no food, so most of the time we ate some of the potatoes that we dug up. We would make a big fire and put potatoes into the fire and then grab one and eat it. It seemed wonderful at the time; we felt we were lucky to have a potato to eat. We had potatoes three times a day.

Those who were judged to be coughing the most severely were sent back to Moscow, but only near the end of our three or four weeks there. It was well into autumn when the rest of us came back to Moscow, and everybody was still coughing. I remember we had a lecture on mathematics with a small bright lecturer who did not think much of us because we were biologists and not mathematicians. He started every lecture with the words, "O…kay,…bi…o…lo…gists!" And he emphasized this word "biologists." We all got cold and trembled from fear He had an awful habit of asking us to stand up to answer his impossible questions. Sure, we could not answer correctly; we were not mathematicians, only biologists. It was torture. And we underwent more torture when we tried to hold our cough, but the cough came out anyway and completely interrupted his lecture. This professor pointed to those who were coughing and said loudly, "You! You who are coughing! Get out of here! Go out into the corridor and cough, then come back." The whole lecture was one interruption after another, people going back and forth.

After a day of this, we found another way. We just crawled under the seats and sat there because it was an amphitheater with no tables, so that if you crawled under the seat, the professor couldn't see you. But he understood what we were doing, and he climbed up the stairs, looking in every row and finding those hiding under their seats, which was not difficult. The professor sent those he found out of the auditorium, yelling, "It's impossible to deliver the lecture with all of your coughing!" We were very sick. I remember that I coughed until spring.

University classes lasted until the end of May, two semesters per year, with five graded exams after each semester and seven or eight pass-fail tests. I always got grades high enough to get a small government stipend, enough to buy something to eat, but not enough to pay for an apartment or to buy clothes. My stipend was thirty rubles each semester, just what a pair of decent shoes cost. A hundred rubles would buy a coat, and a dress was about forty rubles. I spent my stipend mostly on food, and six rubles for a transportation ticket for the bus and subway—a pretty good bargain.

One ruble bought a big tasty dinner at the university canteen, but you could eat there for only thirty kopeks, too. It was not a bad student canteen, probably the best one in the area. There were a lot of spots where, for five kopeks, you could buy soft, fresh rolls with poppy seeds inside and glaze on the outside. I would buy three or four for twenty kopeks, and eat them with tea, and not feel too bad. But as far as I can remember, I was always hungry, as was everybody around me.

On the first floor of the new biology building, there was a spot where you could buy some good rolls, juice and little cakes cheaply. There were many kinds of juice: apple, grape, cranberry, and my favorite—apricot.

Our teacher in organic chemistry asked us at the start of classes, "Now whoever had a little breakfast, please raise your hand." No hands went up. None of us had eaten breakfast before our first class. He used to tell us it was impossible to learn without food, that we were destroying our mental abilities, our health and our stomachs. "You have to have something to digest in the morning because your brain needs energy. We work hard here to understand this material. Without energy, your brain is dead. I'm not sure how smart you are, but you have to eat. Go immediately to the first-floor canteen, and drink a cup of coffee or tea with lots of sugar, please, and have a roll. Then very quickly come back." So we ran to the cafeteria and ate and came back satisfied. This teacher was very smart and taught organic chemistry energetically. He included all the modern advancements. He was my favorite teacher, extremely well liked by us all.

During my first year, I did not live at the University. I had a two-hour commute home each day, spent mostly waiting in line at the stations. Buses arrived at Moscow University every five minutes. There was a twenty-minute ride to Metro Tchopskaya, then a twelve-minute wait until the Kagan car arrived, then on to Taganskaya, then wait in a long line for about thirty minutes until an overcrowded Bus Number 46 came and everybody tried to get in. From there it was a boring 45-minute ride to my station. So I found a way to sleep in a friend's dormitory room two days a week.

My sleeping habits were hard on the other students, because I went to bed by nine and couldn't stand noise or light, whereas my five roommates went to bed late. I would put a pillow over my head, and every time the door opened, I would start shouting from under my pillow, "Okay, please quickly come in, but don't wake me, please! If I awake, I'll never sleep again. Oh, please..." It was so disgusting to listen to my squeaking under the pillow, that they readily did what I asked just to stop my squeaking. People went back and forth talking loudly until one o'clock in the morning, so I had to shout and scream that I was sleeping. Finally, all the students learned to tiptoe past my room. I could hear them asking "Is Lilia here tonight? She is? Oh my God; it's a nightmare." Because nothing could stop me from squeaking, nothing! I wanted to sleep quietly, and I continually fought for this without yielding. Nobody wanted to be my roommate. In second year they assigned only two people to one room in the new building on Leninsky Mountain, and I spent three nights a week there.

10

Collective Farms

I had never ridden a bike before, but I learned at the university camp that we attended each summer. As part of our basic education, we had to pass tests in cycling, horseback riding, canoeing, and motor-biking. We examined the flowers, plants, and animals around us, as well as the birds and their songs. We also passed field tests in basic entomology, biology and zoology. It was very educational and interesting to me.

The first summer, my friend Lucia and I helped each other to pass these tests. We started by trying to master the bicycle. We practiced on a flat path next to a deep ditch of water and mud, because all the other paths were full of roots and rocks. She pushed me and I pushed her, and we rode until we lost our balance and crashed, usually into this trough. We got out dirty and wet, swearing: "Damn these bikes and damn this University. Why are they torturing us?" But we climbed on the bikes again and rode back and forth some more.

Everybody knew that Lucia and I were studying bike together, and they began watching us in our routine. By the end of an hour or two, we were dirty and angry. But nobody laughed at us because Lucia and I would fight anyone, and we could hit pretty well. Eventually we both passed the bicycle test and started horseback riding lessons.

Riding was really fun. The horses were big and fat, chosen for their willingness to put up with students. We rode near a huge field, with a little wooden fence to jump over. The horse had to be saddled correctly, ridden around several times and made to jump without hitting the stupid fence. It was fun. After we felt comfortable, we rode out into the field along the river into a meadow full of flowers. I remember the wonderful smells there, and the sunsets and sunrises.

In the class on the military, we learned to take apart a Kalashnikov rifle and to reassemble it. Lucia and I could do it pretty quickly, but we always had leftover parts. We hid them in our dresses, and then dumped them into the trash. We were not the only ones. Our teacher figured it out after the first week and told us, "Okay, okay. I will give you all a *pass* grade, but you must give me back the spare parts." With fewer parts the guns were easier to take apart and reassemble, and we brought any leftovers to the teacher.

The summer months passed very quickly. On the last day, it was announced that all students had to go to Kazakhstan to help gather the huge harvest of grain; anyone who did not go would not be allowed back to the University. A few students got a "medical release," but all the rest of us went.

All of Moscow University was at the Kazanskaya Station the next morning. Loudspeakers enthusiastically announced that "the second-year student heroes are going off enthusiastically to help on the communal farm," that "their patriotism is extraordinary," and that "it is a great event." I was worried because I had nothing warm to take with me. But we were assured that Kazakhstan was not cold. My cousin Ada got some material and we made a summer dress for my trip to Kazakhstan. There was a special store opened for students prior to the trip, so we could buy things, and I bought a sweater there. But I had no boots, no protection from the rainy weather.

At the appropriate time, the huge doors of the twenty wooden train cars slid open and we were loaded inside. Two rows of narrow shelves were mounted along each wall of the car, enough to bunk sixty-four students. We had a specific name for these shelves in Russia, *nari*, and they existed only in prisons and in this type of train car. There was no place to sit. A large can of water and a ladle had been put in the center of the car. This ladle was tied to the can. Maybe they were afraid that this ladle would disappear, I don't know; there was one ladle for everybody. There was no toilet.

The train ride went on and on for four days. We had nothing to eat except for a few snacks that some of the students had brought. Once a day, the train stopped near a military camp where the soldiers cooked kasha for us, served with a little butter, tea, and bread. They sometimes served a greasy type of macaroni, but never any meat. We were very grateful for whatever they gave us because this meager warm food lifted us out of our total exhaustion.

On the third day, diarrhea started on our train. Because of the lack of water, we were very dirty and could not wash our hands, so the train occasionally stopped in the middle of vast fields, and the speaker announced that the girls were to go to the left side and the boys to the right to relieve themselves. We rushed from the train and into the meadows to make a bowel movement and empty our bladders. Who cares if somebody saw you or not, we were so sick with the diarrhea. One girl had such a bad case that she couldn't stop even when the train started up. She tried to catch up to the train, but failed, so she was left in this field alone. But one of the officials jumped out of the train to be with here. Later they caught up to us. It was a very difficult time because everyone in the open car had diarrhea, with no toilet, no hot water, no tea or medication to stop the diarrhea. It was awful!

Once during this trip, my friend Leona and I were late getting back to our car. We ran after it but were losing ground, so some other students helped us into their car. It turned out to be a car full of law students. They were interesting young men, and we talked a lot. It was a wonderful evening. There was a place to sit, and they had built a little fire on a piece of metal in the middle of the car. They had a guitar and were singing very good songs. And they were talking so politely and so respectfully to Leona and me. One of the lawyers told me I was pretty, but I didn't believe him. I still thought of myself as tall, thin and ugly. He said Leonila was a very unusual name and that I had a very unusual appearance for a Russian. He then said to me, "For a while longer, it will be difficult for you, until you understand that you are very pretty. I know this because I understand women. You are really quite exquisite. You'll see."

I didn't think too much of this because I thought he was trying to hook me like a fish. I generally didn't believe boys at all. In fact, I hated them. I thought the only way to interact with boys was to fight with them, not to trust them. I remembered Victor, the high school star.

My friend Leona fell in love with one of the other students and told me she had decided to follow him to his station. She asked me to come with her. But I decided, "No, not me. I better stay with my fellow biology students." In fact, it was clearly not permitted to go wherever you wanted. I knew Leona would get in trouble over this decision, so I told her I was going back to my car at the next stop. Leona said she was going too, but just to gather her things. She wanted me to go to the officials the next day and tell them she was going to ride in the car with the lawyer students. I agreed, no problem.

When the car stopped four hours later, we jumped out. My friend offered me his phone number and asked for mine, but I didn't give it to him. I said if I decided to call him, I would; if not, sorry. I accepted his phone number, but lost it the next day.

We finally arrived at our destination in Kazakhstan absolutely exhausted. Luckily we were settled with kind German families, who were quite different from the local Russians. These Germans used to live along the Volga in the central part of Russia. But after the war, Stalin relocated them to Kazakhstan. They occupied large villages there, and their houses were solidly built in the old German style, very clean and neat. We were assigned in pairs or threes to German families, and they helped us to stop the diarrhea by giving us chamomile tea.

I lived with a strong woman named Rosa who drove a combine. She called me Hilda, because she said I looked German. She had no children and took considerable care of me personally. I became her assistant on the combine.

We stayed with our German families only as long as it took the officials to clean out a large barn for us to live in. They were afraid to have us live with the German families because there was a great deal of prejudice against Germans after the War, even though these Germans had come to Russia two centuries earlier. Peter the Great had invited them, primarily to teach but also to bring their craftsmanship. Many had lived in Russia for generations and had kept their language, culture, cleanliness, and special style. That's why the officials were not inclined to let us live with them for very long.

They got us all together again in this big barn, girls on one side, boys on the other, with only a sheet hung up to give us some privacy when we changed our underwear. We were rebuilding a local school and were told we had to finish by the end of September. We made large bricks out of straw, manure, sand and glycerin, which we mixed, together in a huge depression in the ground. There was a river nearby. The officials let us swim in this river because it was very hot, and we worked hard. I swam as often as I could and for as long as I could. Everybody knew they could always find me there. We worked and then swam and then worked again and swam some more. It was not a bad time.

We mixed the ingredients together in the depression with long hoes, then shoveled the mixture into huge wooden forms and transported them to the sunny hillside for them to solidify a little. Then we removed the bricks from the form so they could harden and loaded them onto the truck to be transported to the school site.

While we were making these manure bricks, I found a horse in a nearby pasture. I fed her, and she grew to know me and let me ride her without a saddle. "Who can manage horses without a saddle?" I thought. "Only me. No one else could ride her." I was a very good rider, even without a saddle. I kept low on her back and grasped her neck and her mane as we rode.

One day during lunch break, this horse got angry with me for showing off to all the students around the depression with the manure mixture. There were about a hundred students, and I was riding around and using a stick to urge my horse on, when suddenly she raced to the depression and stopped abruptly, throwing me right off into the middle of this thick pond of cow manure, straw and sand. It was a new mix, having just been prepared.

The students standing around burst out laughing because the horse had given me my due, and I got filthy. I stood up slowly, ran to the river, jumped in, and swam off as fast and as far as I could. Eventually, some students came to find me for fear I wouldn't come back, but I did. For the next three or four days, everybody made jokes and laughed at me, but I didn't care. After a while, I laughed too, and they finally stopped. It really was funny.

Most of the time we were very hungry living in this barn. However, there was a forest around us where we used to collect a lot of mushrooms during our breaks. In the evening, we put them on sticks and roasted them over a fire. We marveled at how extraordinarily large and tasty they were. [Twenty years later, we read in the papers that the northern area of Kazakhstan had been irradiated by the nuclear industry. I don't know the details, but I know that the mushrooms were much larger than anywhere else in Russia, and everybody ate them.]

We finished building the school on time, and the village children began attending classes right away. As a result, we were transported to our next job in flat open grain fields about forty miles away. The work there was difficult. Dump trucks delivered the grain gathered by the combine to an open area called a *tok*. The driver emptied the truckload of grain right onto the ground. The first twenty days were sunny, and we shoveled the grain up into the air again and again to dry it. Then we shoveled it onto conveyor belts and up into the truck. Shoveling grain was hard, boring, and dusty, dusty.

Unfortunately, the weather did not always remain clear. When the rains started, the grain got wet and spoiled. For days we shoveled this wet grain into the truck, then drove down to the river and shoveled it into the water. Very impressive!

The rainy days opened our eyes wide. We realized that we were so young and naive and that we really didn't understand anything. "What are we doing here? Why are we doing this? Are we stupid or is a crime being committed here? We agreed to come, yes, but we thought we would be doing something worthwhile." Nobody had an answer, and we watched our efforts go into the river. Without proper storage, without barns and grain elevators, it was a senseless task, without glory, without honor. I was very depressed.

In October, we were sent to another area to work. In groups of eight, we pitched hay into the wagon behind the moving combine and packed it down with our pitchforks. When the wagon was full, we pressed a pedal and the straw fell to the ground in a stack. But the wind blew prickly dust all over us, penetrating every open area of skin. Even though the days were hot, we all wore long-sleeved shirts and pants to close off our bodies as best we could from that dust.

I finally discovered a technique to protect myself. When the wind changed to blow straw directly at me, I jumped off the wagon and ran to the other side and jumped back on again. It was dangerous to do this while the combine was moving, but I was tall and quick. The other girls didn't try.

We had been warned that chemicals had been applied to the grain to keep off the bugs, but we were hungry and ate mouthfuls while drying it. A lot of us got sick, with nausea and vomiting, headache, and muscle cramping. About forty or so of our group were really poisoned. There was no assistance.

One night, holding my stomach because of severe cramps, I reached for the water bucket and it was empty. I was so saddened by this event and said to myself, "Even when you are sick, there is no water." The only reason we didn't die was that we were young and strong.

My aunt, who was a physician, had given me some charcoal tablets before I left for Kazakhstan. She told me the signs and symptoms to watch for and how many tablets to take, but I wasn't listening very closely to her. I just took the package. The charcoal tablets turned out to be a godsend. I took some myself and gave some to one of my friends. She always said I saved her life because, before getting the charcoal, she felt like she was dying. But she swallowed the tablets late at night, and told me that just as the sun was rising, she suddenly felt alive again, and the cramps and nausea disappeared. Mine, too. We really had been very sick. This experience made me sad and bitter.

The only food we were offered on the farm was a type of macaroni pasta with smelly corn oil, probably rancid. I never ate it. I was able to do this because my mother sent me nineteen parcels over the summer. She was the only parent to send parcels. I know I was very surprised when I got the first one, but Mom wrote, "I know what it means to be in Kazakhstan. I am sure there is nothing to eat, nothing to drink." The parcels contained ham and dried sausage, sugar, crackers, even some medications and bandages.

When my first parcel came, we were all excited, and we ate it all very quickly. After the third or fourth parcel, I finally said, "Okay, guys, write a letter to your own parents and maybe we'll survive. My one mother can't feed all of us." I always expressed myself very directly, especially about food. "I am not going to give you any more because I am very hungry. You know? Write the letter."

One of my friends did write a letter home about my parcels. She then began to receive huge parcels, too. Only she and I wrote letters.

As a rule, I shared the parcels with the other girls. When there was bread, we ate it right away. But I did keep my ham and sausage for myself, though sometimes I shared it with somebody close to me. Getting those nineteen parcels was amazing. My mother was very good to us over that summer.

Eventually we emptied the field. That evening we sat in our wagons, all eighteen of us, waiting for what to do next. When we awoke the following day, we found the field covered with snow. We had nothing to keep us warm, and no one came to bring us food or parcels. It was very cold, with no hot water. It seemed that everyone had forgotten about us.

Two of the girls who had boots walked ten kilometers to the closest village to buy us something to eat. They found a store, but there was nothing on the shelves except a little bread and some cigarettes. So they bought the bread and cigarettes and came back. We shared the bread quickly and then looked at the cigarettes. None of us had ever smoked before, but we began to smoke the cigarettes. It was pretty ridiculous; everybody was sick and coughing. Sure, I tried a cigarette too, but I got a terrible headache and was coughing, so I threw it away and said, "Oh no, guys. It's not for me. I'm dying." That was my only experience with smoking.

We waited and waited for someone in charge to come. We didn't know what to do; we just sat around in the barn. Finally, after five days, an official arrived and said we were all ordered back to Moscow. He drove us in the dump truck first to the barn to get our things, and then to the train station.

We rode back to Moscow in normal rail cars where we could sit and lie down just like regular citizens. We even had linen and pillows. No food was served on the train, but at the stations, there were always people selling food, usually boiled potatoes in little bags made of newspaper, hot and ready to eat. In the agricultural areas, people sold pickles and tomatoes and apples, too. So when the train stopped, we jumped out and bought food very cheaply. We had been so hungry for so long that we felt like we were in food paradise.

There were two toilets in this railroad car, a real luxury. The first was for the sixty-four passengers, and the second was reserved for the conductor. It was great to have a toilet, even though it soon ran out of water.

We arrived in Moscow on a snowy, rainy Friday. I was cold and wet and wanted someone to greet me as I got off the train. But my parents were home helping my sister, Svetlana, and her kids. I had a little salary money with me to buy food, and I managed to start my second year at the University on the following Monday, October 15, six weeks late.

11
Completing School (1960)

Life at the university was more interesting in second year, with meetings, discussions, singing, and dance classes in a very large ballroom where we all wore long stylish dresses. At Moscow University, I not only learned biology and parasitology, but I was also well prepared for any kind of social situation. The Moscow University faculty urged us to excel at everything: "If riding, ride well; it driving, drive well, if working or studying, work and study well." I was totally absorbed during both semesters that year.

Our summer classes were at a University scientific station on the northern shore of Russia. All students, no matter what their specialty, had to pass through this University station, and study plant biology, marine biology, and other mandatory courses. The station was very well equipped, with a microscope and everything.

One day they sent us to get some data from a little meteorology station in the dense Taiga forest. We were also to collect mosquitoes from a special trap. Four or five of us headed out on the main trail. At one point we spotted a lot of berries and began to eat them, going further and further off the trail. By the time we had eaten enough berries, especially me, we were lost. I reassured everyone, "Oh, no problem. I read in a book that when you are lost, you climb to the top of a tree. I should be able to see the sea and find the right road back to the station." I very quickly climbed a tree. From the top, I saw the sea and pointed out the right direction.

I was starting to climb down when suddenly one of the girls said, "You can take the top of the tree and bend it down to the ground." I grasped a big branch at the top of the tree and jumped out. But we forgot that it was a northern tree, not a southern tree. The northern trees had no water during the winter and thus were very dry and brittle during the summer.

The branch broke and I fell. I was lucky not to hit any boulders when I landed, because they were strewn all over the ground there. Instead I landed on an old tree trunk lying on the ground, whose insides had been destroyed by ants. The tree trunk broke my fall, and its insides sprayed out all over the area. I hit pretty hard on my head. When I got to my feet, I vomited and got dizzy, probably because I had a concussion. From that moment on, I have had migraine headaches.

Later that summer when we had returned to Moscow, I met a young man named Sasha, a Moscow University student who tutored others for their exams. He was very attractive, smart, and polite. I liked him very much. We walked around Moscow in the evening and talked about everything. We went to some movies together but just as friends. He lived in the center of Moscow, while my house was far outside the city. He told me that he was going to be a journalist; I was studying to be a biologist.

He was tall and black-haired. He was the first young man to say he paid attention to me because of my height. "Your body is proportional, so your height isn't negative. And you have beautiful hair and eyes. I am your friend, so I can tell you this: you are very pretty."

He was not trying to hook me like a fish. When he asked me what my first impression of him was, I said, "I don't know... no impression at all. Boys are boys. But you are polite, which is good, because I don't want to fight with you." This made him laugh. We went to football and basketball games, and he tolerated my loud whistling at the players. Sasha and I became good friends that summer, but then we lost touch with each other.

Before starting third year, we harvested grain in a different area in the south, with no forest at all surrounding the fields. First we worked on the combine gathering the grain, and then dried it by shoveling it into the air. This area was equipped with a few grain elevators and granaries, but the fields were so huge that much of the grain was still wasted. When the rain soaked it, which was often, we dumped it into the river. At least I was not sick when we went back to Moscow. There we learned that our government had bought a lot of grain from Canada that fall.

Moscow University was generally an open-minded place, and Moscow itself was beginning to change a little. A lot of foreign movies began appearing in the theaters around this time. After my third year, a movie called _The Stork is Flying_ became a real phenomenon in Russia. It was a war story of love and betrayal, starring Tatiana Samoleva. The people in my courses began saying, "Leonila Vladimirovna, you are like Tatiana Samoleva, not so much in appearance as in your style." One friend of mine told me about her dream to go to Paris and not come back. I asked her why she felt free enough to tell me this fact which could get her into trouble. She replied, "I noticed that you always resist. And even if you don't say anything, your face shows it."

I had gradually been changing myself. But after this movie appeared, I developed a style and a presence noticed by those around me. My dresses were more European; I was wearing high heels. My hair was still long, but well arranged. I began to enjoy being different. Sure of myself, I knew that I was attractive, like a foreign movie actress. I was not concerned about what people thought of me.

After I had graduated from the University and had started working, I saw Sasha again at a Kremlin ball for young people. We both attended alone, so we danced together the whole evening. We recollected everything; we danced again and again. He said, "It's so amazing to see you, Lilia. You have changed so dramatically. Remember, I told you that you were pretty and would turn into a real beauty? Right now, you are incredible, incredibly attractive." He gave me his phone number, but of course I lost it. But it was okay.

＊

During my childhood in Russia, the Communist Regime worked tirelessly to shatter the souls of my family and me. My brother, sister and I were all children of WWII and its aftermath. My mother and Svetlana were traumatized during the War, constantly worrying not about themselves but about me, my father, and my brother--about our safety in this kind of society. I am so thankful for my father who, in the midst of Communist propaganda and cruelty, treated me so respectfully, taught me the truth, and helped me dream and dare; he fed my adventurous soul. He was a loving teacher, a brave Resistance fighter all his life, a friend and helper to many, many people, a patriot, and a true Russian.

When I graduated from Moscow University and began working, I was prepared to deal with the Communist Party and survive because of all my experiences growing up, and especially due to my mother and father, my sister, Svetlana, and my brother Anatoly. At the end of my childhood in the dreary quicksand of the Soviet Communist Regime, I felt I had emerged as whole as fresh milk.

Acknowledgements

In my first years in America, I wrote down my childhood stories as the memories occurred, and often sent them to family and friends. I want to thank my mother-in-law Elizabeth, for her strong encouragement to keep writing and sending her these vignettes. My husband was tireless in transcribing my letters and audio interviews into an electronic format, then making a first draft of a book to show to people who might be interested.

William Dowie, who has written several books on American writers, and my brother-in-law, Robert Montgomery, a playwright and novelist, both read the first draft and offered their skilled feedback; I particularly appreciated their suggestions of further areas that might be addressed in the book.

My brother Anatoly, while researching his own military books describing the heroic efforts of Resistance fighters against the Germans in WWII, found in the Russian archives pictures of our mother, father, and himself when they were in the Resistance.

The book grew in length slowly, but came to a standstill for many years, until Louise DeVoe Piazza, a friend and memoirist, came to our assistance, and moved the book forward with her observations about additional content, her final editing, and her connections to Opus and the mechanics of self-publishing.

I thank all these people for their support in this effort to bring to the general public a child's experiences living under the Russian Communist regime during and after WWII.

Leonila "Lilia" Montgomery, RN, PhD
June 16, 2018

CPSIA information can be obtained
at www.ICGtesting.com
Printed in the USA
FSHW02n1614300718
50921FS

9 781624 291746